Lloyd Alexander

Lloyd Alexander. Photo by Alexander Limont.

LLOYD ALEXANDER

A Bio-Bibliography

JAMES S. JACOBS
and
MICHAEL O. TUNNELL

Bio-Bibliographies in American Literature, Number 1

GREENWOOD PRESS
New York • Westport, Connecticut • London

Library of Congress Cataloging-in-Publication Data

Jacobs, James S.
    Lloyd Alexander : a bio-bibliography / James S. Jacobs and Michael
O. Tunnell.
        p. cm. — (Bio-bibliographies in American literature, ISSN
0742-695X ; no. 1)
    Includes index.

    1. Alexander, Lloyd—Bibliography. 2. Children's literature,
American—Bibliography. 3. Authors, American—20th century—
Biography. 4. Alexander, Lloyd. I. Tunnell, Michael O.
II. Title. III. Series.
Z8025.6.J3 1991
[PS3551.L35698]
813'.54—dc20
    [B]   90-24515

British Library Cataloguing in Publication Data is available.

Library of Congress Catalog Card Number: 90-24515

ISBN: 978-0-313-26586-0

First published in 1991

Greenwood Press, 88 Post Road West, Westport, CT 06881
An imprint of Greenwood Publishing Group, Inc.

Printed in the United States of America

∞

The paper used in this book complies with the
Permanent Paper Standard issued by the National
Information Standards Organization (Z39.48-1984).

10 9 8 7 6 5 4 3 2 1

CONTENTS

ACKNOWLEDGMENTS

Without the help of the following people, this book would have been impossible to write:
   Lloyd Alexander
   Ann Durell of E. P. Dutton & Company
   Judith Huber of Brigham Young University
   Colleen Martin of Northern Illinois University
   Kemie Nix of Atlanta, Georgia
   Charles Schlessiger of Brandt & Brandt, literary agents, Incorporated

INTRODUCTION

Lloyd Alexander is one of the most respected and best loved of children's authors. He has written and published over thirty books for adults and children and has received most of the major children's book awards. His work has been the topic of at least five scholarly studies, primarily dissertations and theses. Alexander is also noted for his contributions to magazines, anthologies, textbooks and professional journals. Because his body of work and the criticism of his work is sizable, and because of his fine reputation, Lloyd Alexander is an especially appropriate subject for a bio-bibliography such as this.

In order to present as clearly as possible an overview of Alexander's professional and private lives, and to provide an annotated listing of writings both by and about him, this volume has been divided into four sections: Biography, Annotated Bibliography, Appendices, Index.

1. The *Biography* emphasizes Alexander's development as a writer.

2. The *Annotated Bibliography* lists writings by and about Lloyd Alexander and his works. This bibliography is divided into three sections: primary sources, those written by Alexander himself; secondary sources, items written about Alexander; and audio-visual media relating to Alexander.

Primary sources are divided into five categories which have been assigned the following letter codes for indexing:

Books by Alexander
  Adult audience (A)
  Young audience (Y)
  Translations by Alexander (T)
  Foreign editions of Alexander's books (F)

Shorter Fiction by Alexander (S)
Other Writings by Alexander (W)
Illustrations by Alexander (I)
Unpublished Speeches and Writings by Alexander (U)

Secondary sources are also divided into five categories which have been assigned the following letter codes:

Books and Monographs (B)
Dissertations and Studies (D)
Articles and Book Chapters (C)
Book Reviews (R)
Miscellaneous Sources (M)

All **Audio-visual Media Relating to Alexander** are listed together and given a separate letter code (AV).

3. Two *Appendices*: **Awards** and **Lloyd Alexander Chronology**

4. A complete *Index* of names and titles.

Though care has been taken to find bibliographic information and to locate each item mentioned in the bibliography section of this volume, there are instances when a piece of information or even an article or book review remained elusive. These instances are rare, and instead of eliminating an incomplete entry, it seemed a better decision to provide as much of the citation as possible. While it is difficult for a search of this sort to be exhaustive, every effort was made to be thorough.

Lloyd Alexander

BIOGRAPHY

Lloyd Alexander's relationship with books began early. Born in West Philadelphia on January 30, 1924, his first memory of life is a clear picture of sitting with a book and reading. He also remembers spending many hours listening to others read aloud to him. Those memories were confirmed by Alexander's mother and by his only sibling, an older sister named Florence. Both remember his wandering about the house with a book, stopping to ask whomever might be present to please read to him. If unsuccessful, he would retire to some spot and "read" the book himself, dutifully thumbing over each page while retelling the story from memory or deciphering the events from the pictures.

Alexander's early experience with books was not a peripheral part of a day but the most important part of his life, not an occasional activity but the *major* activity. All this contact with books resulted in young Lloyd's learning to read long before he began school. No one recalled with certainty how old he was when he acquired the ability to read, but best estimates put him at age three. He remembers spending at least one hour daily reading by himself as a preschool child, estimating he completed a minimum of two books per week during the two years before school. It is important to keep in mind this reading occurred in the mid-1920s, a time when the picture book was in its infancy. The books he read were not of the variety with generous art and scant text so familiar to toddlers today but were books filled with print and intended to be read by children much older than he.

While Alexander was still very young, his literary appetite was genuinely eclectic, and he devoured all books with equal enthusiasm. This universal appeal of the printed page may be due in part to the volumes available at home. The books in the household library were not many, but they represented an incredible cross-section of reading material. The hundred or so titles comprised a wondrous compost of the wildest conglomeration of gems and junk; Shakespeare and *Warwick Deeping;* Melville and Marie Corelli; something called *The Little Leather Library;* plus a few blurry volumes in imitation morocco, given as inducements by a local newspaper trying to raise the number as well as the cultural level of its subscribers.[1]

Lloyd entered first grade at age five. Of his first year in school, he remembers wanting instead to be home with his books. His years of having been read to and then reading by himself had helped him reach the point where he could read practically anything he wanted. This, he was careful to point out, did not mean he could understand every book in the house or that he did not need occasional help. Yet by the time he started school, Lloyd had personally read about 200 books in addition to the many others that had been read to him. Considering the time spent reading other printed material as well, there is little wonder that the reading activities in an average first grade classroom would not interest him.

During the summer of 1931, the Alexanders moved from West Philadelphia to the suburbs of Drexel Hill, Pennsylvannia. Lloyd entered the third grade that fall, continued to find school not to his liking, and continued to read much on his own at home.

In the fall of 1933, Lloyd was nine years old and beginning fifth grade. During October, while the classes were still new, achievement test scores were received and evaluated. Lloyd and six others in the fifth grade were advanced into the sixth grade as a result of those scores.[2] Because he had started school at age five, one year earlier than his present classmates, the additional year he now gained made him two years younger than the rest.

Lloyd was eleven years old and in eighth grade when he found the library. He had been aware of it years earlier, but the library was somehow not to be trusted. For the first part of his life, all of his reading was done with personal books—some handed down, some bought by assorted relatives. It was inevitable that the day would come when the personal books to which he had access would simply be too limited to give Lloyd what he wanted. This day came during eighth grade, and at that time he forced himself to go to the library in downtown Philadelphia. The experience turned out to be more agreeable than he anticipated. The building itself was surprisingly pleasant, especially the sweeping staircases and marble floors.

While the architecture was appealing, the books were irresistible. While his feet aimlessly walked the aisles, his eyes scanned hundreds and hundreds of titles. That the library was organized into areas of subject matter with a system for locating any specific title did not concern or even interest Lloyd. His system of finding good books had always been to select the most promising book from whatever limited source was available, usually his parents' collection or the library his Aunt Annie had accumulated during her years of teaching and now enjoyed at home. Unlike most people who consult a card catalog or librarian, Lloyd studiously avoided both. Apparently he did not understand how to use the card catalog and had no desire to learn, and his years in school had taught him that librarians are better left undisturbed. His only known method of locating books—look over the possibilities and see what appeals—continued to serve him well here. Even though he was unaware of the Dewey Decimal System, Alexander had a much easier time concentrating his reading in a chosen area because all he had to do was wander long enough, and he would eventually find all of Dickens or classical mythology or whatever, neatly arranged in one spot.[3]

One wonders why he did not make use of the library that served his own community of Drexel Hill. Lloyd was not sure if there was one, if the inconvenience of getting there was too great, or if he just didn't bother since the Philadelphia library was so magnificent. Whatever the reason, the only library he ever visited was the one in the city. Not until senior high did he discover and borrow books from Upper Darby Township's Sellers Memorial Library.

Oddly enough, during all of his trips to the library, the young man who would one day win two of America's prestigious awards for children's books—the Newbery Medal and the National Book Award—never once visited the children's section of the library. He claims not to have avoided it purposely, but simply says he was not aware such a place existed. Lloyd was perfectly satisfied wandering in the general fiction section and reference room, and lived happily in ignorance of an area specifically for young readers.[4]

Lloyd had thought and planned for years concerning his occupation. He first settled upon his life's work around age eight, when his reading interests were centered in classical history and mythology. Fascinated by what he read about the Greeks and Romans, and intrigued by the men who went into archaeological sites to uncover the actual tools, belongings, and homes of the ancients, Lloyd planned in all seriousness to become an archaeologist.

Alexander's next occupational choice was made a few years later. Since the time he was a very small boy, Lloyd had shown an ability and interest in drawing. He was now sketching and painting frequently and well enough that he thought of making art his career. Those who saw his work liked it, and he went on to experiment further with oil and other media in addition to his customary drawing pencil.

The fact that making a dependable living from art was risky did not affect Alexander's choice. Remuneration was never a criterion for judging the desirability of a vocation, especially after reading Romain Rolland's novel *Jean Christophe*. The hero of this detailed, complex story is a Beethoven-like character who clearly shows the anguish, sacrifice, and despair present in the life of one who is dedicated to his art. *Jean Christophe* spoke directly to Lloyd, who believes that books do, perhaps, help teach us our roles in life. He identified completely with the novel to the extent that it seemed Rolland had written his own story. Lloyd Alexander was Jean Christophe, and both could somehow survive the challenges and conquer.

When Lloyd was fourteen, he had an additional insight into his future and selected another occupation. For years he had been a regular church-goer but attended without really knowing why. He sensed some kind of deep fulfillment while at the services in his Episcopalian Church, the Chapel of the Mediator, and these feelings led to his decision to become an Episcopalian priest. This decision was more serious than the others made earlier.

At this time in the 1930s there existed a whole corps of priests who went to poverty-stricken areas to offer help. Once in these desperate locations, the priests engaged in socially oriented work as much if not more than in theological. The duties of a worker priest fit well into Alexander's own religious sense, which was more of the helping hand variety than the theological/philosophical. He saw personal meaning and fulfillment in following the path of the cloth.

The dream of the priesthood faded when Lloyd realized that in order to go to divinity school, one must first have a college education. There was not a chance in the world that Alexander could ever afford college. He had no money. His parents certainly had no money. Although they were pleased with the idea of his becoming a priest, there was nothing they could do to help him with the expenses of a higher education. Abandoning this idea was not easy for Lloyd, yet he could see no other alternative, and the ambition simply played itself out.

Where he made conscious decisions to become an archaeologist, an artist, and a priest, he never decided to be a writer. Writing was not a profession to be chosen; it was a part of life, like breathing. That he would write was a given. Naturally, throughout the time of considering these various occupations, Lloyd wrote regularly—as he always had done. Even when he was small, he invented stories and told them orally, sometimes accompanied by his own pictures. Other stories he illustrated completely in elaborate picture sequences. Once he learned to write, he put down his stories on paper. As he discovered different styles and varied literary genres, he would try these new forms out in his own words.

During the years he was planning for the clergy, he saw a common ground between priest and writer. For Alexander, there was not "any qualitative difference—philosophically, poetically, metaphorically—between a desire to preach the word of God through the scriptures, and to preach the word of God as it preaches itself through art."[5]

Having read W. J. Turner's *Biography of Mozart*, Lloyd understood that Mozart worshipped God as the God of music, and that "Mozart's worship of God and Mozart's creation of music are the same thing." In his mind, Alexander saw himself becoming a priest who could practice successfully both the religion and the art.[6]

In time, the thoughts of other professions became fewer and fewer. What mattered to Lloyd was his writing, and he pursued it constantly. Somewhere in the middle of his high school years, Alexander decided he would concentrate his writing on poetry—not poetry in general, but romantic poetry. To enrich himself and his writing, Alexander was going to fill his soul with the world's best poetry. A general goal was to memorize all the poetry he could; a more specific aim was to commit to memory the entire *Oxford Book of English Verse*, a comprehensive volume of almost 1200 pages and approximately 800 poems. When asked about the success of the undertaking some three decades later, Alexander replied,

A futile project of memorization, impossible! I worked at it off and on for maybe a year. I still do remember chunks of things; e.g., lots of Rubáiyát, Kubla Khan, bits of some Shakespearean sonnets. And a lot more, but maybe in addition to the OBV, I did read other anthologies.[7]

Concurrent with the memorizing of verse was the composing. Alexander spent hours writing verse in the best form of the nineteenth century poets. Before this commitment, he had spent only evenings writing, but now it was not uncommon for him to begin his work in the afternoon. Alexander estimates that he spent an average of five hours a day in this pursuit. *Jean Christophe* stayed with him, and he learned to pay the price of the artist. During these years he wrote hundreds and hundreds of poems, sending many of them to potential publishers without success.

Not long after beginning his concentration on romantic poetry, Lloyd expanded his efforts to include work at the opposite end of the writing spectrum: realistic short stories. He approached these in the then-current Hemingway and Steinbeck tradition of the slice-of-life narrative—the tough, naturalistic story. Every effort was also made to market both the romantic and the naturalistic creations, but nothing was accepted.[8]

Alexander's failure to have anything published should not be seen as that of a hit-and-miss writer who occasionally sent off a piece of his work to a randomly chosen publication. What he undertook, he undertook completely. He was disciplined, put in his hours every day, and mailed his writing off continually. Accurate records were never kept, but Alexander did save his rejection slips, which numbered in the hundreds.[9]

Alexander graduated from Upper Darby High School in June, 1940. With the freedom of graduation came the responsibility of finding a job. Lloyd was not interested in working—he had plenty to do just keeping abreast of his studying and writing—but his father's zeal more than equalled Lloyd's lack of concern. Here was a high school graduate, a potential wage earner who could now become a producer and contributer instead of a consumer and taker. Lloyd had finished with the business of education and must be about the business of finding a job.

What better place than a solid, reputable bank, suggested his father. Lloyd could think of dozens of better places; but with his father's prodding, he applied for a position at the Fidelity Philadelphia Trust Company, one of the city's most proper and respectable. Largely because of his parents' connections, he was hired as a messenger at the bank shortly before high school graduation.

> The messenger force was called The Bench because we sat on one—a massive, leather-covered mahogany plank in a corner of the main floor. Numbered lights, flashing on a call-board, referred to the various departments of the banking area and we took turns answering them, delivering documents throughout the building. Our uniform consisted of an alpaca office coat, cut round and narrow in the shoulders which made even the most athletic clerk look humble.[10]

Alexander hated his job at the bank. He hated the work, hated those to whom he must answer, hated the alpaca coat, and dreaded the thought of being permanently tied to such an institution. He and his father were not soulmates in their outlooks on life. Lloyd was the romantic idealist and wondered how his father could not see the same great and glorious vision of the future. But his father was above all else a practical man whose primary business was to survive, and whose primary interest in his son was to get him into a job with a reasonably secure present and a promising future. The job at the bank undoubtedly filled that bill, but it certainly was not what Lloyd wanted. Since his father was so concerned about his son's employment, since he was instrumental in locating the job, since there was probably nothing else better that was immediately available, and since Lloyd did feel a responsibility to bring home some kind of pay, he resisted the urge to quit. But he would have liked nothing better than to be fired, for then he would be freed of the responsibility of severing ties and would not be to blame.[11]

The one bright spot about working was that Lloyd was earning his own money. He calculated that by living frugally, he could spend a year at college for every year he worked at the bank. The time away from formal education, however, would put him behind the other students. More than ever he needed to keep up his scholarly pursuits in order to keep the gap between him and his future classmates as narrow as possible.

Alexander broadened his reading. To prepare for college, he needed to spend time with all subjects. He studied literature, history, philology, psychology, and whatever else he could. He now spent every evening from about six o'clock until midnight with his books, in addition to whatever time he could find during the day and on weekends. During this time at the bank, he read much of the works of Freud, Jung, and Adler, among others.

Lloyd also found time to write more than ever before, and he continued to send off his works—with the same results he had experienced in high school. The pile of rejection slips grew higher and higher. Finally, he hit paydirt.

The *Writer's Digest* is read by writers and would-be writers. Each year it sponsors a short story contest limited to entries of 1500 words. Lloyd entered the contest at least once prior to 1941, when he again tried for one of the 200 prizes. But in 1941, he garnered 29th place, and his prize ("two cents a word for each and every word in the story") came to $25. He promptly spent it all on books—a collection of Eugene O'Neill's plays, a volume dealing with Sigmund Freud, *Best Plays of 1941*, *Leaves of Grass* and other "substantial things that I read on for months afterwards."[12]

Alexander endured at the bank for 18 months before quitting to go to college. During that year and a half, he not only saved sufficient money for one year's education but also had located a school that seemed to fill his bill. West Chester State Teacher's College had a low tuition and was within a reasonable commuting distance, about twenty miles from his home. He took the placement exams, found out that his scores permitted him to skip many of the usual first year classes, and began his course of study at a weightier level.

If high school had been a disappointment and the bank a disaster, attending college turned out to be the supreme misfortune on earth. The best Alexander can find to say about his classes is that they were "utter tripe and junk." They not only bored him but also made him furious. Expecting to find a rigorous, disciplined atmosphere developed by dedicated scholars on the faculty, he instead encountered teachers who taught watered-down material and wore academic blinders. His classes, which were supposed to focus on material for advanced students, dealt with things he had already digested, in some cases years before; and his teachers were not willing to consider anything outside of their narrow course outlines and equally myopic personal prejudices. The English teacher spent the majority of class time on elementary grammar. The psychology teacher responded to one of Lloyd's comments, which pointed out Freud's view on the matter being discussed, by forbidding him, or anyone else, to ever bring up that reprehensible name in class again. It was plain to Alexander that the academic situation at the school was not Oxford, and it was that type of atmosphere he needed at the time. Perhaps because he started college two years later than others in his class of 1940, Alexander may have felt he was behind and ill prepared for college study. Surely much of his personal studying stayed with him and probably put him at a level above the majority of his classmates who may not have been so dedicated to learning on their own. It seems fair to say that perhaps his discipline and non-accredited curriculum yielded much better results than he had anticipated.

The college experience lasted one term and two days. Even with all of his distaste for the first semester, he decided to give higher education one more chance. Surely all the classes couldn't be as bad as the ones he had the first time around. Only two days were needed with the new set of courses to confirm the lesson learned earlier, and he simply withdrew. There was no need to take time and pay precious money for the "unspeakable intellectual atmosphere" of the school.[13]

The dilemma of Alexander's future was now more complex. Despite the unpleasant experience of public school, Alexander knew he could hang on until graduation when he would be free to follow the pure pursuits to happiness. The time at the bank could be endured for he knew he would never stay there, and it was also providing him with the means to get some of the advanced education he always sought. West Chester State was finally his opportunity for further schooling, but it was sour at almost the first bite. He could not continue there. For the first time, he had nowhere to go and no plans.

Lloyd was still living under his father's roof, and his father still firmly believed in the power of the regular paycheck. Lloyd scouted around and took the only job he could find, which was working in the mail room of the Atlantic Refining Company. It was even less to his liking than being a messenger. At least at the bank he was around and about the building, but at Atlantic Refining his activities were confined to the walls of the company post office. For about six completely uneventful months, he opened mail, wrapped packages, and wondered what to do with the rest of his life.[14]

World War II came to Lloyd's rescue. It had been one year since the Japanese had bombed Pearl Harbor, and the war effort was continuing to grow in both the South Pacific and in Europe. Always a romantic, Alexander now had a cause and a reason for leaving Atlantic Refining. The solution was so perfect he should have considered the army months earlier. By joining up, he could not only postpone having to make serious decisions about his future, but he also could also distinguish himself in the glories of war. That Alexander never had the least inclination toward the battlecry aspect of life made no difference. He was more than willing to enter the action without a doubt that he was perfectly suited to strike a significant blow for victory.

The romantic bubble burst the instant Alexander was sworn in as a soldier in the United States Army. Nothing happened to precipitate the apprehension, but somehow he was flooded with the reality of the situation just as he was raising his hand to take the oath. All at once he sensed that the army was a real organization, and not one of swashbuckling, carefree adventurers but of military bureaucrats who had serious plans for him, some of which he might not like. He simply saw that he "was the last man on an enormous totem pole of absolute authority," and would be completely subject to those who had total control of his life and who were not primarily concerned with his own views on things. In that instant he felt helpless and trapped.

The next few months were a khaki nightmare. To New Cumberland, Pennsylvania, for processing. To Camp Howze, Texas, for basic training. Assignment to a 105 howitzer battery. Reassignment to the camp band as a cymbal player. Further reassignment as a chaplain's assistant, which turned out to be a glorified title for church custodian.

Desperate to find anything worthwhile in the military, Alexander noticed an announcement on a bulletin board for a new specialized training program for personnel who offered the army an acceptable academic skill or specialty. Those selected would take classes at various colleges in the United States. Alexander filled out the necessary paperwork.

Word soon returned that he, indeed, was accepted into the new program. Plucked from his cleaning chores in the chapel and sent to a nameless camp for a brief processing period, Alexander there learned that the school where he would take his academic training for the new position was Lafayette College in Easton, Pennsylvania—about 90 miles from downtown Drexel Hill. The news was almost enough to shake his pessimism.[15] From the misery of menial labor in flat, faraway, sunbaked Texas to a college environment in the beautiful Pocono Mountains near home was the stuff of fairy tales.

The instruction at Lafayette College turned out to be far better than that earlier bought with his own money. The instructors, although under army contract, were all civilians and mostly university professors with specialties in some kind of discipline related to Europe. The fifty students studying mainly French received general instruction in European history, law, and economics, as well as more specialized courses in French politics, geography, customs, and the like. Alexander somehow found a way to expand his personal curriculum to include study in Spanish.

Some of the classes were even exceptional, like the one in French customs taught by a man who had spent the best part of his life in France. In addition to the subject matter, he gave his students a genuine feeling for the country and supplied them with a wealth of valuable and interesting minutiae, such as the name and location of a good restaurant in Lyon and the types of wildflowers to look for in August. Alexander knew vaguely that the information in these classes would be important in his military future, but his appetite for knowledge about Europe in general and France in particular was sufficient motive for him to devour the classroom instruction and devote himself to the homework with little thought to the army's purpose for placing him at Lafayette College.

Alexander's exposure to genuinely interesting knowledge was not his only good fortune at Lafayette. Those who had been plucked from sundry other military installations around the country offered him the kind of satisfying personal interchange that Lloyd had not experienced since his days back in Philadelphia at the bank. Once those who were taking French instruction began to talk among themselves, they discovered many had been misfits in their prior assignments and had more in common with each other than with their earlier companions. It was during this time at Lafayette College that Alexander met Max Jacobson and Ed Johnson-Muller, both of whom would remain his life-long friends and prove to be sounding boards and valuable advisors in his writing career.

After a surprise visit by a stranger wearing no insignia or rank on his uniform who privately interviewed in French the fifty soldiers trained in that language, six were sent to Camp Ritchie, Maryland, for specialized intelligence training. Alexander was in that half dozen; Jacobson and Johnson-Muller were not.

Where Lafayette College offered a strong academic emphasis, Camp Ritchie was all military training. Those selected for this specialized instruction were exposed to a wide curriculum of cloak and dagger skills that would be essential in their assignments with European civilians who were working against the Nazis.

The army allowed six months for Camp Ritchie training. Having arrived in March, 1944, at age 20, Alexander was scheduled to be sent abroad in September. Almost exactly in the middle of this training, on June 5, D-Day took place and changed the course of the war in Europe. Those at Camp Ritchie wondered how this would affect their futures, but the training period continued as outlined. Alexander was promoted to the rank of Technician 3rd Grade (Staff Sergeant with a technical specialty) at its conclusion. Then, instead of being parachuted behind German lines in France to work with the French resistance as planned, Alexander and the other French speakers were sent to Swansea, Wales (near Cardiff), for several weeks before being moved to Lichfield, England, to await further orders. In the army tradition, the group simply cooled its heels for almost two months, their days filled largely with searching for something to do.

Finally, near the end of November, 1944, the Camp Ritchie elite and their jeeps were ferried across the English Channel to France. For almost two years, Alexander had not been a soldier of participation but one of preparation. His time of basic, academic, and intelligence training finally blossomed into a direct contribution to the war effort with an assignment to the 7th Army in eastern France where he spent long days translating radio messages. He spent six months near the front.

In early May, when Alexander's unit had slowly moved almost to Nuremburg, he was sent back to France. He caught a ride on a B-29 and within a few hours was walking the streets in Paris. Because his orders did not specify a time for him to report, he found a place to stay by knocking on doors until he found someone willing to take him in. The next day was May 7, 1945, and Alexander found himself in the heart of Paris on VE Day. After enjoying the delirious festivities, he reported to his new post in the Paris office of the Counter Intelligence Corps (CIC), where he served as a translator and interpreter until the end of 1945.[16]

In Paris, Alexander found Johnson-Muller again. Since the war was over by this time, new opportunities for military personnel were available. One of these was the chance to attend French universities as a part of the continuing education program. Johnson-Muller arranged to have Alexander and himself sent to the Sorbonne, the liberal arts college of the University of Paris. They were transferred to civilian dormitories near the university and were allowed to take whatever courses of study they desired. Not surprisingly, Alexander opted for French literature. Their only connection with the army was their obligation to wear uniforms plus the receipt of military pay. In addition, Alexander received money from a scholarship given him by the French government. He was 21 years old at this time.

In this university-army period, Alexander began to renew his literary interests. During his endless days of translating, he was so preoccupied, and the environment was so oppressive, that he largely ignored reading and writing for the only period of his life. But he now started to visit bookstores and read reviews and literary criticism in French magazines. It was in one of these publications that he first became acquainted with Paul Eluard, one of the modern French poets of great acclaim. After seeing Eluard's name a few times, Alexander was intrigued enough to buy his newest book when it came out, a collection of recent poems.

He did not expect to be so impressed by the poetry. Eluard's credentials and acclaim were not disputed in France but, if anything, Alexander thought them underrated. Eluard wrote poetry the way Alexander wished he had been able to. He immediately bought everything else he could find in the stores.

While reading and re-reading the books, Alexander could not imagine living out his life without meeting this man to tell him what he thought of his poetry, so he called Eluard and wangled a visit. As a gesture of showing what the poems meant to him, Alexander translated a few of them into English and took them along for his first meeting.

Eluard's conversational English was not polished, but he could read the English translations. When he had looked at Alexander's work, his comment was, "It's as if I am reading my own poetry all over again."[17] Alexander then asked if he might translate more. Eluard, in that moment, wrote a letter to James Laughlin, his publisher at New Directions Press in America, telling him that he had found the man who was to be his translator, and no one else. Immediately Alexander began to translate in earnest, returning to Eluard's apartment regularly for the poet to check what he had done and to answer any questions Alexander had. Not only did he approach Eluard for a visit, but he also called upon Gertrude Stein. He simply went to her door and rang the bell. She let him in. He was careful to say that they were hardly good friends, but they did visit at her apartment about half a dozen times for extended periods of an afternoon. Alexander also called upon Picasso (he was on extended vacation in the south of France) and Louis Aragon, a great French novelist. (He was out of town at the time.)

Janine Denni came into Alexander's life during this same time. She and three friends were walking home on the Boulevard Haussmann from an afternoon together when the rain started. At that moment, Alexander and a friend from the CIC office happened to drive by in a jeep. "Not being complete fools, we stopped and offered them a ride,"[18] which Janine refused. With the jeep following along in low gear, the girls ducked in and out of doorways in their vain attempts to keep dry. Finally they accepted the invitation, and "sat on the wet seats in the jeep which had no top."[19]

Despite Janine's promises to herself that she would never marry a foreigner, Lloyd's persistence and charm won over both Janine and her young daughter, Madeleine (called Mado). Janine and Lloyd were married on January 8, 1946.

Along with his studies and translations, Alexander was becoming interested again in his own writing. He knew from simple observation that the majority of his expatriate friends who were planning to stay in Paris after the war spent their days talking about great projects in cafés after having slept late. He, too, was tired after his army experience, and the lulling temptation of the comfortable life was real. It was not that he was weak and would be unable to resist; he was simply weary and sometimes found himself with the feelings of wanting to be tempted. With Eluard's partially completed translation now in hand—the first tangible opportunity to realize his future as a writer—Alexander was concerned for the future. He saw Paris as lotus land. The vision down the road showed that if he continued to eat of the blossoms, he could likely end up joining his late-sleeping friends.[20] Partly because of this apprehension and partly because Alexander missed Philadelphia ("That was my turf, I was used to it."), he had decided upon entering the Sorbonne that he would not remain indefinitely in France.

Janine knew when she married Lloyd that the three Alexanders would eventually return to the United States. She did not know when that trip would take place, but assumed that sometime in the next few years the issue would be faced and all would move to America.[21]

The future was brought sharply into focus with the announcement of a ship taking military dependents to the United States. No one knew when the next ship offering free passage to servicemen's families would depart, but the authorities indicated it would be quite some time. That presented a technical difficulty. If Alexander were to be discharged within the coming few weeks as then indicated, the next vessel would leave when he was a civilian, not a soldier, and there would be some question concerning the eligibility of Janine and Mado's returning with it. If they were going to return relatively soon anyway, missing this boat would mean the family coffers would be tapped for two transatlantic tickets now offered free by the military. All evidence indicated that immediate departure for his dependents was the simplest and most sensible course of action, so arrangements were made. Lloyd would then join them in Drexel Hill after the completion of his present term at the Sorbonne, figuring the cost of his passage to be worth staying until the end of instruction.[22]

When Lloyd returned, the three Alexanders lived in the attic bedroom of his parents' house. His total income was a weekly $20 provided by the federal government to all unemployed veterans for their first year home from the war. For the first time in Alexander's life, a string of entire days—at least a year's worth, thanks to Uncle Sam's generosity—were his to spend on his writing. When Alexander had written previously, he was dealing in hours stolen from a day that largely belonged to something else: attending school and doing homework, presenting himself at the bank each morning, finding significance in college classes, or wrapping whatnot in brown paper and sticking stamps on it in the mail room at the refinery. He now found himself face to face with the future. The time of treading water during the day and stealing snatches of time in the evening and night was gone. He knew he was supposed to become a writer; he had always known that without ever having consciously made the decision. And now the author of promise had the opportunity for which he had worked and waited. His writing, so long granted only a spot in the wings, was now given center stage. A twentieth-century Jean Christophe could certainly deal with adjusting to a new wife who was adjusting to a new country, living in an absurdly crowded home and providing for the needs of a family of three on $20 a week. Rolland's novel about the Beethoven-like character who sacrificed daily and painfully for his art had earlier given Alexander the intellectual blueprint for a life devoted to writing; it now became the actual pattern of his daily living. What mattered was that he had the chance to write something of immediate worth and also lasting literary value.

Alexander began to spend twelve hours each day at his writing. Aware that effort was essential to produce the kind of work he had in mind, he would cut no corners. Even weekends provided no excuse for leaving his typewriter.[23] This unprecedented zeal, while due in part to uncluttered days, was also related to the lack of writing Alexander did during his time in the army. With the exception of a few attempts to write poetry and initial ventures to put together a short story or two, he did not write during the war. For one who had been continually engaged in writing of some sort ever since early childhood—developing elaborate adventure stories, practicing the sonnet form, and agonizing over a short story—to absent himself completely from literary pursuit for a long period of time had resulted in a pent-up desire to compose.

Alexander was greatly encouraged about his future as a bona fide writer. He had time. He had a contract in hand for Eluard's work. Money was imminent when these translations were finished, and a possibility existed that New Directions might have even more work for him. The set-up was ideal. Part of the day, Lloyd could translate, which he enjoyed, and the rest of his time was free to be spent on his own writing. Never before had he been able to work on two projects simultaneously because the creative drain was simply too great. Yet never before had he been given the chance to translate, and translating was more of a mechanical task than a creative effort. He could do both without compromising either.

Lloyd's innocent vision of himself as an artist included an ability to illuminate the mysteries and truths of life in compelling plot and prose. Desiring to do great, deep, moving books that would stun the reader with insight and craft, he had patiently paid the price of preparation to arrive at an "enormous novel of social realism—Balzacian" in scope and feeling.

While that remained his end, there lay in his path an unavoidable literary responsibility. He had lived the hell of warfare first-hand, and it was his duty to put before the world just what it was like to be in France during

World War II. With Jean-Christophe dedication, Lloyd assailed the typewriter for a marathon of 15-hour days. Even the translations were momentarily put aside until the whole story could be told. He estimated his daily output during this period of frenzy to be in the neighborhood of 5,000 words. The book took about ten days from start to finish.[24] With some rewriting, and the addition of a title (*Another Country*—from the Christopher Marlowe line, "But that was in another country, and besides, the wench is dead. . . ."),[25] Lloyd mailed it to Bernice Baumgarten, a New York agent with Brandt & Brandt who had shown some interest in his work, and turned his attention to the world's greatest novel.[26]

Since this work would treat the entire gamut of human experience, he had been deciding upon a setting that would provide a fitting backdrop for the variety of characters needed in his ambitious project. Philadelphia was the final choice, perhaps because Lloyd knew it best. Originally called *Eden*, the book "covered every aspect of the human condition" in all corners of Philadelphia's high society. Alexander explored the meager beginnings of the power barons; walked their paths to riches and glory; delved into the lives of men and women who aided, and hindered, the lives of those in the inner circles; and laid open the intrigue and deception hidden behind the public images of those who ruled Philadelphia and its glittering society. Alexander referred to it loosely as *War and Peace in Philadelphia*, freely acknowledging its scope to be at least as broad as Tolstoy's.

This unwieldy undertaking was not completed as quickly as *Another Country*. While Alexander did not neglect his translations as he had when writing the war novel, the days spent trying to hammer *Eden* into submission rapidly became weeks, and, in turn, grew into months.

Half of the designated year during which Lloyd was allowed to keep his hand in Uncle Sam's pocket had passed when Drexel Hill's struggling young writer took account of his life. He had six more months of guaranteed income. His family had no place of its own to live. He needed continued help from his parents, both with board and room. Despite hopes to the contrary, not a penny had found its way into his pocket from his writing, and no checks were forthcoming in the immediate future. Bernice Baumgarten had not been able to find a publisher for *Another Country*. The Eluard translation was finished, but New Directions had decided to hold its publication. Alexander was asked to translate Jean-Paul Sartre's works: *Nausea*, a novel, and *The Wall*, a collection of short stories. For reasons known only to the publisher, both were to be released before the book of Eluard poetry. Royalties for the translations would be delayed until the finished books were being sold to bookstores and libraries.[27]

Lloyd took a hard look at his immediate future as an author/provider for his family, and reluctantly admitted he would have to search for work. The most painful element of seeking regular employment was not having to face a mindless eight-to-five job every day, but having to admit that the moment he had waited for all his life—the time when he could prove himself with his writing—had not been the success he was sure it would be. Everything had seemed to point toward this as the year of Alexander's triumphant entry into published literature, despite the challenges of Janine and Mado's adjusting to America, poverty, and sardine-like living conditions.

Those shortcomings, in a way, even lent an air of familiarity and authenticity to Lloyd's Jean-Christophe approach to writing. He could accept everything about his sacrifice for art except having to give up before realizing success.

Mechanically he turned to the classified ads, talked to acquaintances, inquired at the bank, and even checked the situation at the refinery. The results were always the same—no job. Post-war America was not crying for workers at that time. The only compensation was that job hunting was not a full day's work. After he had exhausted the day's possibilities, he still had ample opportunity to write.

At that time his sister Florence was taking some craft classes and practicing her skills in the evening. She had bought a potter's wheel and kiln which were in the basement of the family home. Florence had a sure hand and a discerning eye in artistic matters, and shortly after her wheel and kiln were set up, she was producing what were obviously marketable products. The idea of earning money at home was intriguing to other family members besides Flo. Her brother, the boy who received his lowest grades in subjects demanding the use of motor skills, was desperate enough to consider becoming Flo's apprentice. She took him on.

Despite his disappointing performance in shop and gym classes, Lloyd eventually became an acceptable potter. He claimed never to have learned how the clay is centered, but actually did make about twenty marketable ceramic items, mostly bowls and ashtrays, which the Philadelphia Airport gift shop handled for a percentage of the sales. The return was a pittance, however. About four months after beginning the enterprise, the wheel was still and the kiln cold.[28]

Alexander's struggles continued through the remainder of 1947 and into 1948. Nothing promising in either employment or publisher's contracts came his way. He continued his daily writing, and somehow continued to hold his small family together without an income.

Before 1948 ended, he found employment at Sun Oil Company writing advertising copy. *Nausea* was also published same year. With these new successes, Janine and Lloyd bought their first house in nearby Kellytown. It was charming, had a big lot, and was practical. The upstairs could be converted into an apartment to help with the payment.

Three months after moving in, Lloyd was fired. The blow was twofold. First, he needed the money. The most convincing argument for buying a home was that Lloyd's regular paychecks would cover the monthly mortgage. Second, the loss of employment added to his burden of failure. Lloyd had been back in America five years with none of the successes he had envisioned coming much earlier.

The financial problem was alleviated by Janine, who remembered that a neighbor woman had mentioned she could help Janine get a job at the textile mill if the need ever arose. Janine contacted her, went to the mill, and returned as a wage earner. With the apartment rented to an agreeable young couple, part of the monthly mortgage was taken care of; Janine's salary was enough to meet the remainder and keep the wolf from the door.[29]

The problem of what to do to succeed in his life's desire was not so easily solved. Lloyd was out of work for the better part of a year. This time there were no illusions of somehow making a living with his writing.

Lloyd's major concern was to get back on someone's payroll as soon as possible. Most of his time was spent trying to locate another job, but that was not an easy task. He did write—it was next to impossible to completely abandon something that rose up from so deep within—but serious doubts about his ever achieving success in the literary world began to surface. Alexander had always believed that sometime, somewhere, someone would recognize in his work the energy and effort it contained—the enlightenment it surely had to offer. Thoughts now began to creep into his mind that no matter what he tried, he simply was not going to make the grade. For one who always had been sure of his eventual literary victory, these cracks in his faith were indeed serious.

Things would have been different had Alexander not devoted himself so much to his art. Had he been a weekend or occasional writer, there would not have been so much reason for dejection. But that was not the case. Writing was what mattered to him most in life. He had given himself to it completely since coming home from France, and he tried absolutely everything he knew to be successful. He did *not* write haphazardly or without discipline. No one he had ever known tried harder or more consistently. His best was simply not good enough.

Alexander began to lose hope. His agent could find no interested publisher. He admits to having periods of terrible depression, much worse than ever before in his life. The beginning of this difficult period was near the time he was fired from Sun Oil. It continued for another two years.

Of this time, Janine reports that even her best efforts to lift her husband's spirits were all in vain. She would try to lighten his load, to refresh him by taking his mind off his work for a while, but nothing worked. He would want only to stay at the typewriter and continue writing, so she sometimes would leave the house and go to his mother's home for the evening. When she returned, he would still be bent over the machine.[30]

By this time, Lloyd had been working more than seven years without success, and "I had absolutely nothing left, and I was ready to quit." When asked if he genuinely considered quitting or if that statement figuratively reflected his extreme disappointment and despair, Alexander replied, "I considered it the way you would contemplate shooting yourself in the head. I don't know whether I seriously contemplated that or not, but I was ready to."[31]

During one more examination of his writing, after Alexander "had exhausted every possible thing I could say [in my books], all of a sudden I realized that I had overlooked the only thing that I had known anything about, and that was my own adolescence." Almost like a light flashing in his head, he realized "by the process of emotional elimination" that he had never written anything based directly on his own personal experience. He had completely ignored the fact that many authors' first novels centered on their own experiences but had never made the connection in his own life. Alexander felt that writing about oneself "never applied to me. There was nothing to tell about my young manhood. It was the stupidest time of my life, as far as I was concerned." The realizations that his youth was an untried area, and that others had, indeed, used their own experience regularly for subject matter occurred almost simultaneously. This insight came when he

had "reached rock bottom and didn't know whether to laugh or cry." He
started to laugh, although the sound at first was something like "the laughter
of the damned," but it changed into a whopping belly laugh in appreciation of
his own vanity and foolishness.[32]

> I began laughing uproariously at myself as the stupid, presumptuous
> fool. Idiot—you're writing novels of high society. Fool—you haven't
> even crossed the tracks of the Main Line. What are you doing? I
> laughed at myself, and it was very salutary. . . . I think that really saved
> my sanity.[33]

Alexander recalls how he selected the specific topic for his first attempt at
writing after learning how to laugh.

> As a drowning man sees his life pass before his eyes, the former World's
> Greatest Novelist looked back on the events that had brought him to
> such a dismal end. I remembered my first job at the bank; what then had
> seemed catastrophic now struck me as deeply funny. I was able to laugh
> at it, and at myself. Having nothing else left, I wrote a novel about it, my
> fourth and last attempt.[34]

In writing *And Let the Credit Go* (1955), Lloyd attempted to get the
entire feeling of what the messenger experience was like. The novel did not
attempt to explain and enlighten the vast complexities of the human
condition. It focused, instead, upon the messengers, the most humble
employees, of one bank in one city. It centered upon a scant eighteen-month
period. A Jean-Christophe type of thinking would have dismissed this
undertaking as entirely too narrow and limited to reveal anything
worthwhile to a potential reader. Because Jean-Christophe was one of Lloyd's
models, *And Let the Credit Go* was such a long time in coming. It was not
going to be one of the world's greatest novels; it was, in fact, a last ditch effort
before a walk off the pier. While *And Let the Credit Go* violated all of
Alexander's premises concerning what his contribution to literature should
be, it was also the first book of his own to be published. The lesson in the
experience was not lost on Alexander.

> If our failures teach us more than our successes, I had ample opportunity
> to learn. During those seven years, I had undertaken great cosmic
> themes, explaining What It All Meant when I myself hadn't the faintest
> idea. Now, instead, I learned to write about things that I knew and
> loved, that were meaningful not in some abstract sense to some
> hypothetical writer, but to me as a human being.[35]

Alexander learned more than the importance of writing about the
familiar. In thinking about this new approach to writing, he realized that
instead of dissecting things with a meat cleaver, one can use a scalpel. It is
possible to be just as incisive with wit and laughter as with the grim, dour,
life-is-real, life-is-earnest approach. As he pondered this new revelation, he
saw that his recent discovery was hardly new.[36]

I should have known it all the time. . . . I had had examples in front of me all my life. Jonathan Swift: I had only to reread *Gulliver's Travels* to realize that it was hysterically funny as well as scathing and vitriolic. Swift was doing what he wanted to do with a razor blade. George Bernard Shaw: I saw in his writing a constant use of this approach.[37]

While Lloyd had set his writing career on an entirely new track, he basked in the success of his first published novel, giving little thought to his next book until the day a salesman representing his publisher came to Philadelphia. In an effort to increase sales and exposure, it is not uncommon for a sales representative to squire a new author to various book stores in the writer's hometown, which is precisely what this salesman did to Lloyd. At the end of the handshaking day, the salesman turned to the new author and asked, "Well, what are you going to do next?"

Lloyd called that inquiry "the fatal question." Anyone can do one book, but the second one is the killer. He had considered the possibility of that problem arising during his day with the salesman, but claimed he had thought of no answer. In the moment when the issue was raised, on the spur of the moment without knowing what possessed him, Alexander answered, "I'm going to surprise you. I'm going to write a book about my cats." The salesman was pleased.[38]

Later Lloyd knew why. Animal books are very popular and good sellers. Almost like cook books, they are a staple and move very well. The young man's first novel is a risky business with an unknown writer pushing an unknown story. Alexander had seen during that day the difficulty a new author of fiction has when the book is marketed. When the two approached a buyer to promote the new book, the buyer wanted to know what it was about. Alexander reported seeing "the chill set in" when the salesman tried to explain how it was based upon this man and his experiences as an adolescent. Hardly a solid commodity. But if a book is about horses or flower arranging, or something identifiable, people are more eager to deal with the book.

The next day a telephone call came from Bill Poole, Alexander's editor at Crowell, encouraging Lloyd to get going on the manuscript so a contract could be written. That call clinched his commitment to the book, and *My Five Tigers* (1956) began to take shape in his mind. As Alexander thought seriously of writing a book with his cats as subjects, he began to realize just how many authors of note had written about their pets. Thomas Mann

wrote a charming, beautiful book about his dog. Michael Joseph, the great English publisher, wrote several books about his cats. Carl Vandechten, a writer from the 1920s, wrote a classic book on cats called *Tiger in the House*. Even Mark Twain wrote a memoir about a cat he knew. I discovered that this was not a silly thing to do, but was a real, legitimate subject which other people had treated superbly. This is the kind of book I want to write. It's not going to be an idiotic, *My Friend, Catty*. I wanted to do a personal, affectionate, loving book about my animals which meant a great deal to me.[39]

With an eye born of love, Lloyd observed the characteristics of the feline world in general and each of his tigers in particular. *My Five Tigers* remains one of the easiest books he has written. The material had been refined daily since the arrival of his first cat, and "the book wrote itself" in about eight months.

After ten years of serious writing, Alexander seemed to be finding the right combination. Lloyd had published two books and wrote every night on what seemed to be good bets for future publication. His work day continued to be spent in downtown Philadelphia. After his year of unemployment in 1952, he found work as a proof reader—copy editor, and then quit after a year to become a proof reader—copy editor—layout artist. Alexander's next position called for even more of his drawing ability: He added "cartoonist" to his resume.

While at this last job, Alexander completed the remaining four books he would write for adults. Of the four, two were largely autobiographical, *Janine is French* (1959) and *My Love Affair with Music* (1960), and two had nothing to do with Alexander's immediate life, *Park Avenue Vet* (1962) and *Fifty Years in the Doghouse* (1964).

Janine is French is a light but very frank look at the adjustments of a native Parisienne upon emigrating to the United States as a war bride. Alexander has said *Janine* is almost purely autobiographical. He is careful to add, however, that a portion in the magnitude of one percent is not true, and cautions that one should not underestimate the influence and limits of that one percent. The same caution applies to *And Let the Credit Go* as well as *My Love Affair with Music*, which is ostensibly about music, "but actually it's a pretty complete and reasonably accurate biography."[40]

Park Avenue Vet and *Fifty Years in the Doghouse* came to Lloyd through his agent Carl Brandt, a New Yorker who was also a cat lover. (Bernice Baumgarten, his former agent, left the firm and was replaced by Brandt). Brandt's veterinarian, Dr. Louis Camuti, limited his practice exclusively to cats, and subsequently became famous among New York City's cat people. Dr. Camuti treated a number of cats belonging to well-known personalities, automatically charming owners as well as patients in the process, and had collected endless stories about people and cats through his years of practice. Carl told Camuti and Alexander about one another, suggesting they get together in the name of their common feline bond. During the meeting, he suggested they might consider the possibility of writing a book together.

All went according to Brandt's hopes. Camuti and Alexander collaborated on a book, which they published as co-authors. *Park Avenue Vet* is Louis Camuti's story with Lloyd serving as a technician/craftsman in helping him get it all down.

The writing of *Fifty Years in the Doghouse* was similar to *Park Avenue Vet*, at least regarding Alexander. Members of the American Society for the Prevention of Cruelty to Animals in New York evidently saw Camuti and Alexander's book and contacted Carl Brandt to see if Lloyd would be interested in writing the history of their organization. Lloyd accepted the assignment to write what he called a "pot boiler," viewing the work as more a journalistic exercise than anything else. Yet he did not see it as anything lesser, only something different. His challenge as a writer was still there: "To take the particular subject and get as much of yourself into it as possible. In other words, to make it a personal thing. If a writer can internalize the subject, that can become the difference between a work of competent craft and sincere interest, and a work of hackmanship."[41] In working toward that end, Alexander spent much time with William Ryan, the central figure of the ASPCA and founder of the organization. He taped Ryan during their interviews, and Ryan himself put much more information on tape, mailing it to Lloyd. Alexander made a number of trips to New York, visiting ASPCA headquarters and parts of the city where episodes occurred he was detailing in the book. And Lloyd, again, haunted the library.

> It wasn't good enough for me to take one of Ryan's humorous anecdotes about an elephant on the loose, or whatever, and simply retell it. I tried to inform myself about the biology of elephants—to give myself as much background as I could, whether I used it or not. The book had to come from somewhere I knew. . . . To develop any understanding of a man's work with animals, you have to understand the animal as well as the man.[42]

Alexander bought books about animal behavior and animal psychology; he went to encyclopedias and zoological reference books for months before beginning the actual writing. He estimates he read 200 books in preparation to write his own. The information he dug up fascinated him, and, he is sure, contributed to a better book as well. He holds no false notions about the greatness of the book—or about the other he wrote on assignment, for that matter—but said if he were going "to write a pot boiler, it was to be the best pot I could produce. My pride was in doing them with the type of professionalism that I like very much."[43]

Alexander's most prolific writing has been for children, although he neither began with children's books nor had them as his goal. He actually began to write for children during the same time he was writing his adult novels by accepting two commissions from the Jewish Publication Society, which was seeking writers to produce juvenile biographies of historical Jewish personalities. From a list of possible historical figures, Lloyd selected the name of August Bondi because of his Civil War connections. Alexander had "always been fascinated by the Civil War."[44] For six months, Alexander collected and sorted information for the book, which he viewed as a "challenge . . . and wonderful training." Writing *Border Hawk: August Bondi* (1958) was an enjoyable discipline yet "a work of craft rather than a work of art. I tried to do my best at it, to make an external assignment mean something to me as well as meeting the terms of the contract."[45]

Alexander was proud of the result. In 1959, it was honored by the National Jewish Book Award, given annually to the best children's book on a Jewish theme. Alexander then finished *Janine is French* and *My Love Affair with Music* before accepting another commission. In 1960, two years after *August Bondi*, Alexander's name appeared on another book published for the Jewish Publication Society—*Flagship Hope: Aaron Lopez*. Lopez, a

Portuguese Marrano who left for America to avoid religious persecution, was born and lived most of his days in the eighteenth century.

Alexander's next book, *Time Cat* (1963), was different from all earlier titles in three ways. First, it was the first novel "where the impetus came from my own viscera." Second, it was Alexander's first fantasy. And third, it was the first book he consciously chose to write for a young audience. Even Alexander himself was not entirely sure why he shifted to the children's book form.

> I had been writing for adults (in the case of two biographies, for "young adults") with great satisfaction and modest success. But, at that particular point in my life, for reasons I still don't altogether understand, I felt that I wanted to write a book for children; that whatever it was I wanted to say could best be said, or could only be said, in that form.
>
> The initial difficulty, unfortunately, was that I hadn't the vaguest notion of what I wanted to say. . . . For some while, I lived in a state of confusion and perplexity, seasoned with recurring doubts as to whether I should even embark on a project so different from any I had done before. An external event finally clarified my internal bewilderment.
>
> One of my favorite cats, Solomon, had the habit of sidling into my work room to pass the time of day. . . . But he had a way of padding in so quietly that I was never aware of his arrivals; he was simply there. After we finished our games and conversations, he would drift out as silently as he had come, and I was never sure I had actually seen him leave.
>
> I laughed to myself over this. As part of the mythology pet owners build up around their pets, it pleased me to imagine Solomon had the gift of appearing and disappearing at will. Pushing this a little further, I speculated where he might go when he chose to vanish.
>
> The answer I gave myself was that he was exploring other places, perhaps even other times. If a cat has nine lives, does he have to live them one after the other? Supposing they were all available to him, he could go visiting any of his various lives, whichever happened to appeal to him at a given moment.
>
> Solomon was luckier than I. The way things were going with me, in my one life as a writer, made me envy his multiple existence. I wished he would take me along on his expeditions.
>
> Having indulged myself in this diversion, I put such idle fancies from my mind and went back to brooding over my lack of an idea.[46]

The idea, of course, eventually came, and Alexander wrote about the visits of a cat named Gareth to nine different countries in history, taking along Jason, his boy owner. In order to do a credible job of believably handling Jason and Gareth's visit to a country of antiquity, Lloyd returned to the library to do research on each of the countries the two were going to visit. He called this time of laying groundwork something "like looking at words in a dictionary. One thing leads to another." He read books on history, anthropology, sociology, folklore, catlore, and the "Daily Life in Peru" orientation—more than 60 titles in all to prepare for creating realistically detailed backgrounds of the countries to be visited.[47] (He justified the number of titles as being "a small number compared with the extensive scholarly research a largescale historical novel or biography requires.")[48]

Alexander discovered his "tremendous gold mine of fantasy" while engaging in this research. In a book since forgotten, he discovered that "St. Patrick was not Irish, but was actually Welsh, and his name in Welsh meant 'Good Cat.'" This piece of information intrigued Alexander and seemed to be enough of a rationale to write one episode based on Jason and Gareth meeting a young man named "Good Cat."[49] Lloyd also discovered that long before St. Patrick became St. Patrick, he was kidnapped from his native Wales and taken to Ireland by Irish slavers. A natural story, thought Alexander.

> Jason and Gareth run across this young boy with a strange name, the future St. Patrick, of course. They meet him in Wales, probably in some spot where I had been myself. I can draw on my own sense of the country because I know it and am fond of it. What could be more natural than this? . . . They all get kidnapped by these Irishmen in a big dramatic scene. . . . The easiest thing in the world to do.[50]

While Alexander concentrated on Wales to collect sufficient information to write this chapter, he found more than he bargained for.

> Surely everyone cherishes a secret, private world from the days of childhood. Mine was Camelot, and Arthur's Round Table. . . . The Welsh research brought it all back to me. Feeling like a man who has by accident stumbled into an enchanted cavern lost since boyhood, both terrified and awestruck, I realized I would have to explore further. Perhaps I had been waiting to do so all these years, and some kind of moment had come.[51]

Alexander could not ignore the things that

> began stirring inside my head. Strange, personal stirrings began to happen to me. This was far too rich a thing to do in one chapter, so I changed my idea. Instead of having Jason and Gareth meet St. Patrick in Wales, they meet him in Ireland, and it becomes an Irish episode.[52]

Time Cat was finished with no mention of Wales. But immediately upon its completion, Alexander turned his full attention toward that source of his stirrings.

Without knowing the purpose, Lloyd began reading Welsh mythology and folklore. The book that interested him most was the *Mabinogion*, the canon of Welsh mythology. Unlike other mythologies that read with a great degree of clarity, the *Mabinogion* is "the common body of ten or eleven tales that appear in two somewhat romantically named medieval Welsh manuscripts, the *White Book of Rhydderch* (written circa 1325) and the *Red Book of Hergest* (circa 1400)."[53] As such, it is often disjointed, confusing, and has little internal cohesion.

Despite the lack of satisfying form, Alexander was drawn to the images and incidents of the *Mabinogion*, as well as to its appealing flavor. The book was personally stimulating; it also offered the haunting possibility of something else to Alexander. He was not sure precisely what.

> My first intention was to base a fantasy on some of the tales in the *Mabinogion*, and I started to research accordingly. However, I soon found myself delving deeper and deeper into the legends' origins and significance; searching for what exactly I didn't know—to the despair even of the librarians, who must be among the most patient people on earth. A historical-realistic approach did not work. Unlike the Irish and Norse, the Welsh mythology has been irreparably tampered with, like so many pictures, old and new, cut apart and pasted every which way.[54]

Alexander continued to reread the *Mabinogion* (he estimates a minimum of twelve thorough readings), in addition to pouring over whatever related books he could locate, like Robert Graves' *The White Goddess*, "a study of Welsh poetry filled with fascinating things like the secret alphabet of the bards."[55] While still wondering what was to come from all this, Alexander kept extensive notes on his readings.

> Sifting the material, hoping to find whatever I was groping for, I accumulated box after box of file cards covered with notes, names, relationships, and I learned them cold. With great pains I began reconstructing a kind of family tree or genealogical chart of mythical heroes. (Eventually I found one in a book, already done for me. Not in the first book, but in the fifteenth!)[56]

It was during this process when Lloyd first met Ann Durell, the editor at Holt with whom he had been working. Alexander's agent, Carl Brandt, decided that editor and author finally should meet after months of contact only through the mail, so he suggested a dinner in New York for five—two Brandts, two Alexanders, and Ann Durell. The evening, pleasant and relaxed, offered an ideal atmosphere for conversation. Lloyd used part of his to tell Ann about "this wonderful Welsh thing he was going to do." She listened as he described in detail what could come out of his *Mabinogion* study; her suggestion was that he give the story further form by including "some sort of real protagonist the reader can identify with, perhaps a boy or girl." In a later communication, she changed the recommendation to include "two human characters (boy and girl) of your own devising to make a bridge for the reader."[57]

Lloyd continued to read and take volumes of notes, but the reading and note taking had its limits.

> The trouble with research is: all you end up with is research. At a certain point, you have to stop reading and start writing, and somehow transform your data from antiquarian curiosa into a story. . . . A good example of the kind of material I had to struggle with was a fragment from a book called the *Myvyrian Archaiology*; it turned up often in the other research, too, and for some reason so stuck in my mind that I kept

going back to it again and again. It describes a certain battle in only about half-a-dozen lines that go, in part, like this: "And Arawn King of Annuvin fought. (Annuvin is the Celtic Hell or Underworld.) And there was a man in that battle who, unless his name were known, could not be overcome. . . . And there was a woman called Achren . . . and Gwydion ap Don guessed the name of the man."

Those few lines eventually gave me the plot framework for *The Book of Three*.[58]

Ann Durell offered Alexander a $1000 advance when he signed the contract for the first of the planned books.[59] By December 20, the contract proposal and manufacturing estimate were completed for a trilogy tentatively called The Sons of Llyr. Holt, Rinehart and Winston estimated the manuscript deadline for October 1, 1963, for the first book, which was to be called *The Battle of Trees*. One year later, October 1, 1964, *The Lion with the Steady Hand* was due; the last book, *Little Gwion*, was to be delivered to the publisher on the same date in 1965. Each book was estimated to sell for $3.95, be 192 pages long, and have twenty line drawings. Holt planned 10,000 copies of each title in the first printing and expected to sell 6,000 in the first year.[60]

While Alexander recalls the creation of the book as arduous, he remembers one early part of the writing as especially troublesome.

I recall clearly the birth of one particular character; in this case, a difficult delivery.

I was groping my way through the early chapters with that queasy sensation of insecurity that comes when a writer doesn't know what's going to happen next. I knew vaguely what should happen, but I couldn't figure out how to get at it. The story, at that point, needed another character; whether friend or foe, major or minor, comic or sinister, I couldn't decide. I only knew I needed him and he refused to appear.

The work came to a halt in mid-page. I couldn't go on. I couldn't by-pass that section and write around it, since future action depended on what happened now. Day after day, for better than a week, I stumbled into my workroom and sat there, feeling my brain turn to concrete. In the course of my research, I had come across an eighteenth century account of the various characters in Celtic mythology. One had stuck in my mind: a creature described only as half-human, half-animal. I had hoped this would give me a clue; but Gurgi, as the text named him, was no help to me.

One morning, I went to my workroom for what had become a routine session of sniveling and handwringing. Gurgi still refused to enter the scene. I could see him vaguely in my mind's eye, but I couldn't hear him. If only I could make him speak, if only I could catch the sound of his voice, half the battle would be over. He kept silent.

I sat there, expecting to pass the morning as usual, crying and sighing. Suddenly, for no apparent reason whatever, I heard a voice in the back of my mind, plaintive, whining, self-pitying. It said: "Crunchings and munchings?"

And there, right at that moment, there he was. I could hear his speech pattern, the rhymed phrases that would be his badge of identity. I could see him now, sniveling and wringing his hands, utterly woebegone. Part of him came from research. The rest of him—I have a good idea where that came from.[61]

Initial response to the manuscript was ecstatic, even in letters not meant for Alexander's eyes. Brandt told Ann Durell that he was excited about it, to which she replied: "My first reaction was at last, at last America has produced a writer who's a challenger for the great allegorical fantasy crown, worn for so long by the British."[62]

The editing process lasted almost six months from the first "strenuous deletions" to the final careful readings. One reason Alexander's working title, *The Battle of Trees*, may have been changed is the battle of the trees took place in the first fifty pages of the manuscript, which eventually were deleted. The dragons flying about and other mood images made for a sluggish beginning to the actual story of the protagonist Taran's desire to become a hero. Alexander agreed that the battle, along with other information in that section, did not strengthen the book. He even used Ann's suggested sentence as the new opener: "Taran wanted to make a sword."[63] But agreeing with his editor did not cancel all the pain of seeing one's creation flung into the wastebasket.

Lloyd did not accept all suggestions for changes. After the manuscript was delivered and after hammering out some rough spots with Ann, she wrote him about making the names of the protagonists, Taran and Eilonwy, somewhat easier for the future readers of the books. As a substitute for Eilonwy, she suggested "Branwen." Alexander's reply follows.

15 December, 1963
3847 Dennison Avenue
Drexel Hill, Pa.

Dear Ann:

My poor tender head! Have been cracking it ever since we talked, and have come up with some thoughts about titles, which are attached; and some thoughts about names, which follow.

Concerning Taran and Eilonwy, I'll start with my conclusions; then, more or less incoherently, try to analyze my reason.

First, I think we should keep those names.

This comes after much hard thought, and retyping some passages using a variety of other names. In the process, some observations occurred to me. See if they seem valid to you.

1. Aside from the mechanics—Branwen being a little close to Hen Wen, etc.—the typical Welsh names are indeed obviously and self-consciously Welsh. A little too obvious. Like naming a German "Fritz" or an Irishman "Pat."

2. The easily identifiable names in current usage suffer for that very reason. There is no sense of remoteness or strangeness. They don't taste right to me, and they lose the mood.

3. On the other hand, any good, colorful or gutsy name will be even more difficult. Taran, to me is simple, easy on the eye and tongue. It

seems almost foolproof to pronounce, but even if you mispronounce it you can't hurt it. Same goes for Eilonwy. (Here I do admit some personal bias, I'm sort of fond of it.)

4. As far as immediate identification and recall go, I think a name works in both directions. Sometimes you can strike on an absolutely perfect name that sums up everything about a character (and I sure wish I could think of them). But just as often the name acquires its emotional freight through association and exposure to the story. In isolation, Tolkien's "Frodo" doesn't do much. Same with a great many others. Is "Long John Silver" good per se—or does it fit so well because we know him so well? I don't know.

5. I have a hunch that kids accept and adapt very quickly even to the most outlandish names, and even get a charge out of them.

6. Here's an entirely personal point, but I add it for what it's worth. In some weird way I've got used to those names. Changing them, as I tried valiantly to do, turns Taran and Eilonwy into different people and total strangers. It would take one hell of a wrench to reorient myself. I suppose I could if I had to, but I'd rather not.

Didn't mean to go on at such length. But I didn't want you to think I'm being stubborn or lazy, or infatuated with the book as it is. I'm in favor of anything to improve it, and any way to improve it is certainly worth the effort.

Do let me know what you think.

See you soon.

Lloyd

P.S. Checked with Taran and Eilonwy themselves. For once, they both agree: "Don't change our names!"[64]

The letter also illustrates, at least in part, the degree of attention Alexander gives to detail.

Carl Brandt summed up what those who worked with the book felt about it. After receiving a copy of the finished product, which had finally been titled The Book of Three, the entire text of his letter to Ann read: "I think that the Lloyd Alexander is the most beautiful book I have seen in the juvenile field indeed ever. My congratulations and thanks."[65]

The planned trilogy had come to be known by the general name of The Chronicles of Prydain, and the second book, The Black Cauldron, was written with relative ease. Originally scheduled to appear in the fall of 1965, it was released instead in the spring of that year.

By now Lloyd knew that three books were not enough for the telling of this story. A fourth would be needed to flesh out the tale and draw everything neatly together. He began the third, now named The Castle of Llyr, aware that the fourth and final book, The High King of Prydain, would follow.

During the writing of this third volume, Alexander was working downtown during the day as the associate editor of the Delaware Valley Announcer, an industrial magazine. The office was in the center of Philadelphia, not far from the library and a park, and Alexander used to spend his lunch hour walking about in the downtown section wherever the spirit happened to move him. During one lunch hour foray, he happened past a construction site where a large building was being razed. Lloyd watched the huge wrecking ball swing back and forth for a while, meandered back to work, and gave the incident no further thought. The next morning's newspaper contained the story of how a wrecking ball on a downtown demolition job had snapped its chain and fallen to the sidewalk. Alexander looked more closely at the accompanying picture and saw that it had struck the precise spot where he had paused to observe the goings-on.[66]

Reading about the snapped chain was, indeed, a sobering experience for Lloyd, who felt there was much more at stake in his life at that moment than ever before. Should his number come up very soon, Prydain and all who lived there would remain an unfinished saga. No literary heir, no matter how sincere, could ever get Taran and Eilonwy to the end of their journey by the proper route, the one in Alexander's head.

With the responsibility of creation weighing heavily upon him, Lloyd turned immediately to writing book four, the conclusion of the Chronicles. His aim was to outline the events as quickly as possible, bringing the story safely to its conclusion. Then, with the permission of time and the Fates, he would return in due order to the hastily written volume to revise and refine it for final publication.[67]

All was not well with *The High King of Prydain*, the fourth and last book so hurriedly hammered out to preserve the story. Although it would not appear in print until after *The Castle of Llyr* was completed, Ann reviewed the new book anyway and made her notes. Something was not right, but she could not put her finger on it. She turned the situation over and over in her mind. The book read well enough; the problem was not with style. The characters had completed their development satisfactorily, and the ending was excellent. But somehow the book needed major attention.

Ann went to bed on a Friday evening in August, 1965. At 2:00 a.m. she suddenly awoke with what seemed to be the solution to the problem: An entire book was missing between *The Castle of Llyr* and *The High King of Prydain*. Allusions were made in *The High King of Prydain* to Taran's period of maturing, which occurred between books three and four but was never detailed in either volume. It needed to be developed more fully for the reader. At the end of *The High King of Prydain* (later to be shortened to *The High King*), Taran chose to remain in the world of mortals, rejecting the offer to return to the eternal peace of the Summer Country. The reader needed to feel more deeply his connection with the common folk of Prydain. In short, Taran was "the link between the faery and the mundane" and needed to be established more firmly in the mundane.[68]

Ann's suggestion made sense to Lloyd, who saw that part of the complete story was indeed missing—but only on paper. He had written the entire saga of Taran in his head, including the missing years when Taran had wandered about the countryside of Prydain, unconsciously completing his education while searching for his identity. Alexander was keenly aware of Taran's solitude and frustration during that period, as well as the deep kinship he developed with the people of Prydain, but had not felt it necessary to chronicle those years for the reader. The effects of his wanderings were important, not the wanderings themselves. On the diagram Alexander drew which showed the relationship of all books dealing with Prydain, his hand-printed note indicated the last volume would begin three years after *The Castle of Llyr* ended, leaving that time period unmentioned and unexplained.

Convinced that the reader would benefit from a closer look at Taran's development during these three years of growth, Alexander began to fill them in immediately after finishing *The Castle of Llyr*. He completed the new fourth book, *Taran Wanderer*, just a month after the publication of *The Castle of Llyr* and mailed the manuscript to Ann on May 9, 1965.

The original three books now had become a series of five titles: *The Book of Three* (1964), *The Black Cauldron* (1965), *The Castle of Llyr* (1966), *Taran Wanderer* (1967), and *The High King* (1968). In addition, two picture books about Prydain were written during the same period: *Coll and His White Pig* (1965) and *The Truthful Harp* (1967), both illustrated by Evaline Ness. Alexander's original deadline for completing the trilogy was October 1, 1965. When he delivered the manuscript for *The Truthful Harp* in July, 1966, he had passed the initial deadline by only nine months but had written a total of seven books instead of three. In order not to glut the market, and also to allow time to be sure everything fit together flawlessly, the books were still released one per year with the exception of the picture books. *The High King* appeared in 1968 and, in 1969, received the John Newbery Medal, awarded annually by the American Library Association for the most distinguished contribution to children's literature.

Describing in a speech the meaning Prydain had for him, and the experience of finishing the last book, Alexander said:

> Coming to the last page of *The High King* was a sad moment for me, a feeling more akin to loss than liberation; as if something one had loved deeply for a long time had suddenly gone away. Yet, it was a loss with more than equal gain. Throughout the writing of the book, and even from the first of the five books of Prydain, I believe I had a glimpse of what it felt like to create something; of how it felt, if only for a moment, truly to be a writer. Now, perhaps, I can start being one. Certainly no work has given me greater joy in the doing; and writing for children has been the happiest discovery of all.[69]

After finishing The Chronicles of Prydain, Alexander began his usual six months of post-publication regeneration. During this time, he still rose between 3:30 and 4:00 a.m. but read and pondered instead of wrote. Prydain was finished and published, but Alexander's ponderings could not leave it completely alone. "There were things kicking around in my mind that I wish I had covered in the books. I had the vague notion to do a kind of appendix or a collection of short tales which would finally explain certain minor details in the books I had passed over."[70]

As Lloyd listed eleven possible tales and began to consider working on them, *The High King* won the Newbery Medal. The award stopped any further work on the stories because he did not want "to give the impression that I was trying to cash in on something." Although the book was conceived and begun before the medal was awarded, "I couldn't put a little note in it saying, 'I thought of this book before. It is not trying to take advantage of any publicity.'"[71]

At some point during those six months, a scene came to his mind's eye—a non-rational but emotionally charged picture that needed much refinement and about which many questions needed to be answered.

I saw this eighteenth century young man with his friend . . . in front of some kind of Viennese palace going up a flight of steps. It seemed to make no sense to me, but there was an attitude about it. I had a feeling from it, a gallantry involved. Beyond that I can't say because it was completely incoherent. But it seemed to stick in my mind, and part of the work was justified then.[72]

With that picture and feeling, Alexander began his exercise in "externalizing and rationalizing the irrational sensations, emotions and attitudes . . . which is the 'art work' one must do to make sense out of chaos."[73] Admitting that "it is very hard to describe this process," Alexander gave examples of questions he probably asked himself at the time.

All right, if they're walking up some steps of a weird place, whose steps? Why are they there? What are they doing? What kind of life goes on there? I saw the extremes of poverty, the high nobility, and the slums of Vienna. A woman's face flows in. There has to be a heroine.[74]

Identifying the process as "trying coherently to explain a complete incoherency," Alexander continued to ask questions and get a feeling for the entire scene, not just his limited view of the men going up the steps. When the focus eventually reached critical mass,

I know that this young rascal is a fiddler. I know that, and I know that he is going to have a certain type of bad time, at least to some extent, and I know where it's going to happen. I get a flavor of the period. In short, when all these details—almost an infinite number—start packing up together and the feeling begins to take up a kind of weight, I am aware that it happens, and I sit down and make very rough notes.[75]

Lloyd explained to Ann what he had in mind for the new book.

Now—as to the possible ingredients for this stew: A completely invented country, an eighteenth century Somewhere (i.e., in a completely invented world, as a matter of fact—I mean, there will be *no* countries in this world called England, France, etc. My God, this is a staggering thought in itself! A world made up from whole cloth!) If Prydain's literary ancestors were the *Mabinogion*, King Arthur, etc., this would have an aroma of Tom Jones, Jean Christophe, Mozart, Paganini, Dean Swift, etc. and ad lib.

The possibility for the characters is fabulous. The hero a young man, a violinist and excellent instrumentalist, maybe even a composer eventually. A pure white cat. (Great! Maybe deaf, since all-whites are deaf? Or can only hear certain things?) One main heroine, of course, but maybe also a couple other sub-heroines of differing personalities. Big potential for a lot of great, very human characters and types—aristocrats, peasants, theatre people maybe, townsfolk, provincials and sophisticates. A junkman-ragpicker (he still keeps intruding) might be important. Also scientists and philosophers.

Backgrounds—palaces, slums, elegance, squalor, countrysides, etc.

Possibilities for moods unlimited. Comic, tragic, sad, miserable, absurd, etc. Chance for very great depths of feeling. Much more so, in its way, than Prydain.[76]

Further refining in Alexander's mind yielded a much clearer picture, a blending of the original idea concerning discovery, loss, and the physical elements from the scene with two men going up steps.

The background is early Eighteenth Century—Mozartian, Viennese, rooted in the madrigal, but completely fantastic. There is no such place in the world. But in the sense that the Prydain works are premedieval, this is early Eighteenth Century, with the nobility and the private officers and the common people and the conflicts and the elegance and the squalor.

So the main character is, of course, a violinist. He starts out as a young man with this great facility. In other words, he's a good fiddler, he can play, but he hasn't really "heard." It's all technique. And at a certain point something happens, and it has to do with a violin. He starts getting caught up in the deeper things behind music, and becomes utterly hooked, committed to it. Now, this has fatal—or near fatal— consequences.

So this was no literary exercise for me, but a very personal kind of book.[77]

The writing of what became The Marvelous Misadventures of Sebastian (1970) did not flow in the same smooth channel as My Five Tigers and The Black Cauldron, which were written and accepted with relative facility and ease. The draft of this book was slow in coming, and, when finished, was rejected.

I'd been working on Sebastian for almost a year—just about finished it. Thought I'd finally reached the pinnacle of success. What could go wrong now? I had a skulking suspicion something was wrong, but sent it to my editor, Ann Durell. She said, "No good. It doesn't work!"

At first I was shook up. I was tempted to try to get by with it. But I decided to do the decent and honorable thing—go back and write it again. Neither Ann nor I knew what was wrong. I took a year more and did improve it, but I was still not satisfied.

At this point I found out what was wrong: we know things in our mind that we don't put down on the page. For example, I knew Sebastian was freedom-loving and hated tyranny; but I neglected to include a scene where he actually comes into conflict with despotic government officials. I knew he was brave, but had no major incidents where his bravery was really put to the test. So I rewrote for the third time.[78]

After three massive rewritings, *The Marvelous Misadventures of Sebastian* was released in 1970, winning shortly thereafter the 1971 National Book Award. Alexander did not publish another longer work until 1973, when *The Cat Who Wished to be a Man* appeared. He was not idle during the interim years, as two picture books testify—*The King's Fountain* (1971) and *The Four Donkeys* (1972).

The impetus behind each of those picture books did not come from Alexander. In the case of *The King's Fountain*, Lloyd was preparing for a trip to California when he received a call from Ann Durell asking if he could come to New York the next day to talk with Ezra Jack Keats. Ann engineered a meeting with the purpose of artist and author collaborating on a book, and the idea worked.

The Four Donkeys, illustrated by Lester Abrams, had entirely different origins. Ann Durell moved from Holt to E. P. Dutton & Company soon after the publication of The Chronicles of Prydain. Her former post was filled by George Nicholson, who contacted Lloyd, probably at the prompting of someone in the area of reading skills or reading programs, to see if he could write a story that would demonstrate the use of literary viewpoint to young readers. From that practical beginning came the tale of the donkey and the craftsmen.

The Cat Who Wished to be a Man (1973) came about as a result of Alexander's "personal demons" that periodically beset him with doubt and despair. During these times, it is not uncommon for him to semi-seriously believe that human beings leave much to be desired. Better to be born a cat or a guppy.

As Lloyd began to play with the idea of humanity's misery, he began to see an interesting situation dealing with the response of an innocent animal to the everyday disasters so familiar to humans. The idea intriguing to Alexander was of a reasonable animal suddenly face to face with the conceptions of war, money, violence, and other aspects of life that can whittle away at one's humanity. Yet, early in the planning stages, he saw that he would be able to write an optimistic story.

Despite my wretched demons, who keep nagging at me, my basic position is that as bad as it may be, humanity has something going for it. The faults of humans are outweighed by their virtues.[79]

Lionel the cat was granted his wish to become human. In his adjustment to the world of people and their generally appalling ways, he managed to discover that optimistic truth: Their virtues were even greater than their faults. *The Foundling* came out the same year as *The Cat Who Wished to be a Man*. These stories of Prydain, which predate the tale told in the five volumes, were conceived earlier but abandoned because of the attention brought to Prydain by the Newbery Medal. What gave rise to the book was a new editor at Holt, George Nicholson, who wrote Lloyd to see if he had anything in the hopper. George's letter touched off Lloyd's earlier longing to add to Prydain. Figuring enough time had passed so "the curse was off this by now," he rummaged through the attic, found the old notes, and set to work. The original eleven stories were reduced to six, and Prydain was now as complete as it was going to be.

In 1975, two years later, *The Wizard in the Tree* was published. *Wizard* was not an easy book for Alexander to write. Originally he had planned a much longer work, but he reevaluated after trying "half a dozen drafts and finally realizing that I couldn't do it that way. I had to adjust my sights to what I was capable of doing."[80] The irrational stirrings which eventually took shape as *The Wizard in the Tree* were connected to further meddlings by Alexander's personal demons.

> Call it a mid-life crisis, or whatever, I was physically and mentally ready to cash in my chips. I was in the midst of an awful depression, as bad as anything I've gone through. I felt that everything had fallen apart, and that nothing I had done amounted to a damned thing.[81]

Arbican, the wizard of *The Wizard in the Tree*, had been locked up in a tree trunk for hundreds of years. When finally released by Mallory, Arbican discovered that his magic was no longer working as it should. He was old, out of touch, and his "creative power was botched up and failing."

A case can be made for parallels existing between fictional Arbican and real-life Alexander.

> Try as I may, and I indeed tried my best, there is a gap between the conception and the execution. This is one of the key ideas for any work of art, this gap between the conception and execution. The smaller the gap, the greater the work. The larger the gap, the more unsuccessful the work, whether it is a book, a piece of music, or a painting.
>
> I couldn't close that gap to my satisfaction as far as I privately, secretly was concerned in *The Wizard in the Tree*. I was unsatisfied with it and wish I could have done better. It's very possible, and I hope this is the way it works out, that the kids who read it—and the adults, too—will nevertheless enjoy it. It is not a disaster, but I wish I had written a better book.[82]

Alexander did not have similar struggles with *The Town Cats*, which the critics indeed thought a better book. Published in 1977, Alexander knew two years earlier that this work would be a collection of tales about cats rather than a novel. He did not know, however, what kind of tales they would be. As he thought about the possibilities, he considered three different types: 1) the "how and why folktale," such as how the cat learned to see in the dark, or why a cat bushes out its fur; 2) the beast fable, particularly the beast fable used as a foil to play off human characteristics; 3) the folklore or mythology of cats, such as the parliament of cat leaders that secretly meets each year.[83]

After toying around with the different styles of tale, he settled upon the first. It did not work. The second idea took, however, and Alexander developed two goals for these beast fables. The first centered upon the individual style of each story. The aim of each tale was to suggest a different distinctive style of folk art—Perrault, Italian High Baroque, and so on. The second goal

> was to spotlight the folly, foibles, unreason, and general lack of common sense among humans. The cats are, in that sense, metaphors for reasonableness. Each tale is not only a different folk style; but, I think more important, each tale takes up a particular foible: obstinacy, egotism, pretention, etc. The human characters either show such foibles themselves or are victims of them.[84]

Alexander delighted in polishing the tales and was uncharacteristically pleased with the results. Generally the completion of a work is not a happy time for him because he sees the flaws, concentrates upon the shortcomings, and believes that the finished work is of dubious value. In this case, Lloyd did not think the completed manuscript was all that bad.

His next book, *The First Two Lives of Lukas-Kasha* (1978), is "set in a fantasy world that relates to the primary world of Fifteenth Century Persia." To prepare himself for the tale of a beggar who was transported temporarily to a nameless middle eastern country where he becomes a prince, Alexander read widely in Persian literature—fairy tales, mythology, Omar Khayyám and dozens of other books. He also "looked at Persian miniatures, trying to get that mind set that would allow that secondary world to become very natural for me."[85] Among the many Alexander titles translated into foreign languages, *The First Two Lives of Lukas-Kasha* was his first book to win an award in translation—and it received two: The Silver Slate Pencil Award in Holland and the Austrian Book Award in Austria.

The Westmark trilogy (*Westmark*, 1981; *The Kestrel*, 1982; and *The Beggar Queen*, 1984) marked a departure from Lloyd's traditional focus in writing. For the first time since he began to write for children, his story contained no fantasy. Set in an invented country with the flavor of eighteenth-century France, the books maintained a feeling similar to fantasy even though nothing in them violated the natural laws of this world. Instead, the Westmark trilogy became Alexander's opportunity to treat some favorite themes with uncompromising honesty: the brutality and senselessness of war, how oppression bruises the gentle spirit, and how even the mildest individual must sometimes fight against an oppressor.

Working on these books exacted its toll from Alexander, who "spent a number of very difficult years working on [them]. . . . And having spent such a long time going through such a profoundly disturbing and painful emotional experience, I wanted to relax and have fun, which everyone is entitled to do. I wanted something that would, in effect, heal my spirits."[86]

The search for fun and healing lead him to consider "those preposterous, Victorian melodrama/adventure stories, which I dearly love."[87] As he remembered childhood pleasure in this literary arena, he thought of Rider Haggard, Conan Doyle, Sherlock Holmes, and Dr. Watson. And soon Vesper Holly began to take shape, a teenage, red-haired, humane, decisive, "brilliant genius who always triumphs and always beats the villain."[88]

Alexander points out that the Vesper Holly series (*The Illyrian Adventure*, 1986; *The El Dorado Adventure*, 1987; *The Drackenberg Adventure*, 1988; *The Jedera Adventure*, 1989; and *The Philadelphia Adventure*, 1990) marked a number of firsts for him.[89] *The Illyrian Adventure* is his first fiction for young readers told in first person, the first told by a narrator, the first realistic enough to state a definite year (1872), and the first to have a real location (it began in Philadelphia). The others followed a similar pattern, with the last adding four more firsts: the first to take place entirely in a real place (Philadelphia and its environs), the first to contain an historical event (The Centennial Exposition of 1876), the first to contain actual historical figures (Dom Pedro II, Emperor of Brazil; President Ulysses S. Grant; and Alexander Graham Bell), and the first to offer further information in an author's explanatory note.

Lloyd Alexander has become one of America's most important contemporary authors of books for young readers. Since his first published novel in 1954, he has written 32 books—an average of not quite one per year. Alexander's works have won critical acclaim as well as a devoted readership. He has garnered a host of awards, both at home and abroad. In America, his recognition includes the Newbery Medal (1968 for *The High King*), the National Book Award (1971 for *The Marvelous Misadventures of Sebastian* and 1981 for *Westmark*), the Catholic Library Association's Regina Medal (1986) for his contribution to children's literature, as well as the Helen Keating Ott Award from the Church and Synagogue Library Association (1987) and the Pennsylvania Library Association's Carolyn W. Field Medal (1987). International awards include the Dutch Silver Slate Pencil and the Austrian Book Award (1981 for *The First Two Lives of Lukas-Kasha*); Sweden's prize for meritorious contribution to children's literature, the Golden Cat Award (1984); and the Norwegian Children's Book Prize for *The Town Cats* (1987). He has also received citations from Drexel University (1972), the Pennsylvania School Librarians Association (1976), Keystone State Reading Association (1982), the Pennsylvania House of Representatives (1985), and Villanova University (1990).

Coming attractions include a wryly comical modern folktale called *The Fortunetellers*, a picture book illustrated by Trina Schart Hyman, that is scheduled for publication in 1992. Alexander is now writing a new high fantasy novel. As usual, he is secretive about the content but does say it has an oriental flavor. He even hinted the setting might carry the feeling of eighth-century China.[90]

Alexander continues to practice the rigorous work habits acquired soon after returning home from France. He still rises by 4 a.m. each day, either to prepare for future writing projects or to work on a book in progress. With his writing routine firmly established, and with a wealth of stories still untold, Lloyd Alexander's work is far from done. And his place as an author of distinction is clear, perhaps best defined in a statement to him written by the children and staff of the Chicago Public Library in 1982:

> You are our Harper: Balladeer of the Kingdom of Fantasy. Forgive us, the cruel masters, who demand you work for our pleasure. All we can do is love you as a reward—and we do.

Notes

1. Alexander, Lloyd. "A Personal Note by Lloyd Alexander on Charles Dickens." *Top of the News*, 25 (November 1968): 10.
2. Primary Class Record, Public Schools of Upper Darby Township, Pennsylvania, 1933-34.
3. Alexander, Lloyd. Personal interview with James S. Jacobs, Drexel Hill, Pennsylvania, 16 August 1975.
4. Alexander, Lloyd. Personal interview, 16 August 1975.
5. Alexander, Lloyd. Personal interview with James S. Jacobs, Drexel Hill, Pennsylvania, 20 August 1975.
6. Alexander, Lloyd. Personal interview, 20 August 1975.
7. Alexander, Lloyd. Letter to James S. Jacobs, 6 July 1976.
8. Alexander, Lloyd. Personal interview, 20 August 1975.
9. Alexander, Lloyd. Personal interview, 20 August 1975.
10. Alexander, Lloyd. *And Let the Credit Go.* New York: Crowell, 1955, p. 5.
11. Alexander, Lloyd. Personal interview, 20 August 1975.
12. Alexander, Lloyd. Personal interview, 20 August 1975.
13. Alexander, Lloyd. Personal interview, 20 August 1975.
14. Alexander, Lloyd. Personal interview, 20 August 1975.
15. Alexander, Lloyd. Personal interview with James S. Jacobs, Drexel Hill, Pennsylvania, 21 August 1975.
16. Alexander, Lloyd. Personal interview, 21 August 1975.
17. Alexander, Lloyd. Personal interview, 21 August 1975.
18. Alexander, Lloyd. Personal interview, 21 August 1975.
19. Alexander, Janine. Personal interview with James S. Jacobs, Drexel Hill, Pennsylvania, 20 August 1975.
20. Alexander, Lloyd. Personal interview, 21 August 1975.
21. Alexander, Janine. Personal interview, 20 August 1975.
22. Alexander, Lloyd. Personal interview, 21 August 1975.
23. Alexander, Lloyd. Personal interview, 20 August 1975.
24. Alexander, Lloyd. Personal interview, 20 August 1975.
25. Alexander, Lloyd. Letter to James S. Jacobs, 30 September 1975.
26. Alexander, Lloyd. Letter to James S. Jacobs, 11 February 1975.
27. Alexander, Lloyd. Letter to James S. Jacobs, 6 July 1976.
28. Alexander, Lloyd. Letter to James S. Jacobs, 6 July 1976.
29. Alexander, Lloyd. Personal interview, 21 August 1975.
30. Alexander, Janine. Personal interview, 20 August 1975.
31. Alexander, Lloyd. Personal interview, 20 August 1975.
32. Alexander, Lloyd. Personal interview, 20 August 1975.
33. Alexander, Lloyd. Personal interview, 20 August 1975.
34. Alexander, Lloyd. Untitled, unpublished chapter on fantasy written for Dr. Shelton Root, University of Georgia, 1972, p. 7.
35. Alexander, Lloyd. Untitled, unpublished chapter on fantasy, p. 7.
36. Alexander, Lloyd. Personal interview, 20 August 1975.
37. Alexander, Lloyd. Personal interview, 20 August 1975.
38. Alexander, Lloyd. Personal interview, 20 August 1975.
39. Alexander, Lloyd. Personal interview, 20 August 1975.

40. Alexander, Lloyd. Personal interview, 20 August 1975.
41. Alexander, Lloyd. Personal interview, 20 August 1975.
42. Alexander, Lloyd. Personal interview, 20 August 1975.
43. Alexander, Lloyd. Personal interview, 20 August 1975.
44. Alexander, Lloyd. Personal interview, 20 August 1975.
45. Alexander, Lloyd. Personal interview, 20 August 1975.
46. Alexander, Lloyd. Untitled, unpublished chapter on fantasy, p. 13-14.
47. Alexander, Lloyd. Personal interview, 21 August 1975.
48. Alexander, Lloyd. Untitled, unpublished chapter on fantasy, p. 16.
49. Alexander, Lloyd. Personal interview, 21 August 1975.
50. Alexander, Lloyd. Personal interview, 21 August 1975.
51. Alexander, Lloyd. "The Flat-heeled Muse." *Horn Book*, 41 (April 1965): 141.
52. Alexander, Lloyd. Personal interview, 21 August 1975.
53. Evans, W. D. Emrys. "The Welsh Mabinogion." *Children's Literature in Education*, 9 (Spring 1978): 17-33.
54. Alexander, Lloyd. "The Flat-heeled Muse." *Horn Book*, 41 (April 1965): 142-143.
55. Alexander, Lloyd. Personal interview, 21 August 1975.
56. Alexander, Lloyd. "The Flat-heeled Muse." *Horn Book*, 41 (April 1965): 143.
57. Durell, Ann. "Lloyd Alexander: Newbery Winner." *School Library Journal*, 15 (15 May 1969): 2066.
58. Alexander, Lloyd. "Truth about Fantasy." *Top of the News*, 24 (January 1968): 171-172.
59. Durell, Ann. Memorandum to Mr. Cady, 1 November 1962.
60. Trade Department Contract Proposal, Holt, Rinehart & Winston, 20 December 1962.
61. Alexander, Lloyd. Untitled, unpublished chapter on fantasy, p. 26-27.
62. Durell, Ann. Letter to Carl Brandt, 2 October 1963.
63. Durell, Ann. Letter to Lloyd Alexander, not dated.
64. Alexander, Lloyd. Letter to Ann Durell, 15 December 1963.
65. Brandt, Carl. Letter to Ann Durell, 20 July 1964.
66. Alexander, Lloyd. Personal interview, 21 August 1975.
67. Alexander, Lloyd. Personal interview, 21 August 1975.
68. Durell, Ann. Letter to Lloyd Alexander, 23 August 1965.
69. Alexander, Lloyd. "Newbery Award Acceptance." *Horn Book*, 45 (August 1969): 379.
70. Alexander, Lloyd. Personal interview, 22 August 1975.
71. Alexander, Lloyd. Personal interview, 22 August 1975.
72. Alexander, Lloyd. Personal interview, 20 August 1975.
73. Alexander, Lloyd. Personal interview, 20 August 1975.
74. Alexander, Lloyd. Personal interview, 20 August 1975.
75. Alexander, Lloyd. Personal interview, 20 August 1975.
76. Alexander, Lloyd. Letter to Ann Durell, 29 September 1967.
77. "SLJ Meets Lloyd Alexander." *School Library Journal*, 96 (15 April 1971): 1421-1422.

78. Stuart, Dee. "An Exclusive Interview with Lloyd Alexander." *Writer's Digest*, 53 (April 1973): 34.
79. Alexander, Lloyd. Personal interview with James S. Jacobs, Drexel Hill, Pennsylvania, 22 August 1975.
80. Alexander, Lloyd. Personal interview, 22 August 1975.
81. Alexander, Lloyd. Personal interview, 22 August 1975.
82. Alexander, Lloyd. Personal interview, 22 August 1975.
83. Alexander, Lloyd. Telephone interview with James S. Jacobs, 4 April 1978.
84. Alexander, Lloyd. Letter to James S. Jacobs, 11 February 1978.
85. Tunnell, Michael O. "An Interview with Lloyd Alexander." *The New Advocate*, 2 (Spring 1989): 92.
86. Tunnell, Michael O. "An Interview with Lloyd Alexander." *The New Advocate*, 2 (Spring 1989): 88.
87. Tunnell, Michael O. "An Interview with Lloyd Alexander." *The New Advocate*, 2 (Spring 1989): 88.
88. Tunnell, Michael O. "An Interview with Lloyd Alexander." *The New Advocate*, 2 (Spring 1989): 89.
89. Alexander, Lloyd. Personal interview with Michael O. Tunnell, Drexel Hill, Pennsylvania, 20 August 1989.
90. Alexander, Lloyd. Telephone interview with James S. Jacobs and Michael O. Tunnell, 24 May 1990.

BIBLIOGRAPHY

A. PRIMARY SOURCES

1. Books by Lloyd Alexander

a. Adult audience

A 1. *And Let the Credit Go.* New York: Crowell, 1955.

A largely autobiographical account of Alexander's first job after high school as a messenger in a large downtown Philadelphia bank.

A 2. *Fifty Years in the Doghouse.* New York: Putnam, 1964.
Foreign editions: British, German.

Through the experiences of William Michael Ryan, Special Agent No. 1 of the American Society for the Prevention of Cruelty to Animals, this commissioned book gives an overview of the ASPCA on its fiftieth anniversary.

A 3. *Janine is French.* New York: Crowell, 1959.
Foreign editions: British, German.

Account of Janine Denni's adjustment to America after leaving France as the war bride of returning serviceman Lloyd Alexander.

A 4. *My Five Tigers.* New York: Crowell, 1956.
New York: Dutton, 1973 (paper).
Excerpts from *My Five Tigers* in *My Cats and Me: A Journal with Illustrations and a Space for Notes.* Philadelphia: Running Press, 1989.
Foreign editions: British, Dutch, Swedish.

Warm and detailed view of the first five cats to share the Alexander household.

A 5. *My Love Affair with Music.* New York: Crowell, 1960.
Foreign editions: British, German.

Alexander's musical history from the first discovery of the family piano to his present passion for the violin, with details about lessons, school instruction, concerts, the guitar, the ocarina and his devotion to Mozart.

A 6. *Park Avenue Vet.* New York: Holt, Rinehart and Winston, 1962.
(Joint author with Louis J. Camuti.)
Foreign editions: British, German.

As-told-to account of a Manhattan veterinarian whose practice was limited to treating cats of New Yorkers.

b. Young audience

Y 1. *The Beggar Queen.* New York: Dutton, 1984.
New York: Dell, 1985 (paper).
Foreign editions: Danish, German, Swedish.

Third in the Westmark trilogy. Theo, Mickle, and their comrades make a final stand against the archvillain, Cabbarus, in order to assure freedom for their land.

Y 2. *The Black Cauldron.* New York: Holt, Rinehart and Winston, 1965.
New York: Dell, 1969, 1980 (paper).
London: Collins Armada, 1973 (paper).
Foreign editions: British, Danish, Dutch, Finnish, French, German, Hebrew, Italian, Japanese, Norwegian, Portuguese, Spanish, Swedish.

Second of the Prydain Chronicles. Taran and his companions undertake a quest to locate and destroy the Death-Lord's cauldron, source of his deathless warriors.

Y 3. *The Book of Three*. New York: Holt, Rinehart and Winston, 1964.
New York: Dell, 1971, 1978, 1980 (paper).
London: Collins Armada, 1973 (paper).
Foreign editions: British, Danish, Dutch, Finnish, French, German,
Hebrew, Italian, Japanese, Norwegian, Portuguese, Spanish, Swedish.

First of the Prydain Chronicles. Taran chafes for adventure but gets
more than he bargains for when he and his companions must save
Prydain from the evil Horned King.

Y 4. *Border Hawk: August Bondi*. New York: Farrar, Straus and Cudahy
and Jewish Publication Society, 1958.

Biography of a freedom-loving Viennese boy who emigrated to
America where he championed the abolitionist view and fought with
John Brown.

Y 5. *The Castle of Llyr*. New York: Holt, Rinehart and Winston, 1966.
New York: Dell, 1969, 1980 (paper).
London: Fontana Lions, 1977 (paper).
Foreign editions: British, Danish, Dutch, Finnish, German, Hebrew,
Italian, Japanese, Norwegian, Portuguese, Swedish.

Third of the Prydain Chronicles. Eilonwy is kidnapped by Achren, who
seeks the power of Llyr to rule Prydain. Taran and companions search
the Isle of Mona to find and rescue the princess.

Y 6. *The Cat Who Wished to be a Man*. New York: Dutton, 1973.
New York: Dutton, 1977 (paper).
Foreign editions: Dutch, German, Japanese, Swedish.

When Lionel the cat's desire to become human is granted, he finds
more surprises as a man than he bargained for.

Y 7. *Coll and His White Pig*. New York: Holt, Rinehart and Winston,
1965.
New York: Holt Owlet, 1965 (paper).
Foreign editions: Dutch, Japanese.

A Prydain picture book. Before the days of Taran, Coll ventures into
the Realm of the Land of Death to rescue Hen Wen, the oracular pig.

Y 8. *The Drackenberg Adventure*. New York: Dutton, 1988.
Foreign editions: Dutch, German, Swedish.

Third of the Vesper Holly adventures. Vesper and Brinnie are invited
to Drackenberg's diamond jubilee celebration only to find their
archenemy, Dr. Helvitius, fueling a plot to destroy the duchy's
independence.

Y 9. *The El Dorado Adventure.* New York: Dutton, 1987.
       New York: Dell, 1988 (paper).
       Foreign editions: Dutch, German, Japanese, Swedish.

       Second of the Vesper Holly adventures. Vesper finds she owns a
       volcano in tiny El Dorado. Evil men seek to acquire her land and
       destroy the primitive Indian tribe that lives there.

Y10. *The First Chronicles of Prydain.* London: Fontana, 1986.

       Includes *The Book of Three, The Black Cauldron,* and *The Castle of
       Llyr.*

Y11. *The First Two Lives of Lukas-Kasha.* New York: Dutton, 1978.
       New York: Dell, 1982 (paper).
       Foreign editions: Danish, Dutch, German, Hebrew, Norwegian,
       Swedish.

       Lukas is magically drawn into a new world where he finds himself
       hailed as King of Abadan. His life is soon endangered by powerful
       rivals, and he flees the palace accompanied by some strange traveling
       companions.

Y12. *Flagship Hope: Aaron Lopez.* New York: Farrar, Straus and Cudahy
       and Jewish Publication Society, 1960.

       Fleeing the Inquisition in 1752, Duarte Lopez came to Rhode Island
       where he eventually owned a fleet of merchant ships and fought
       against the British in the American Revolution.

Y13. *The Fortunetellers.* New York: Dutton, forthcoming.

       A poor carpenter never realizes that the carefully phrased predictions
       of a fortuneteller are not at all authentic, yet when he is mistaken for a
       fortuneteller himself, the same predictions bring him fame.

Y14. *The Foundling and Other Tales of Prydain.* New York: Holt, Rinehart
       and Winston, 1973.
       New York: Dell, 1982 (paper).
       Foreign editions: Danish, Dutch, Swedish.

       A collection of short stories about the mythical realm of Prydain that
       predate the story of Taran from the Prydain Chronicles.

Y15. *The Four Donkeys.* New York: Holt, Rinehart and Winston, 1972.
Foreign editions: British, Dutch.

A modern fable in picture book format telling of three tradesmen who travel to a fair. How they get along and respond to the unforeseen reveals not only their own folly but also offers insight into humanity as a whole.

Y16. *The High King.* New York: Holt, Rinehart and Winston, 1968.
New York: Dell, 1969, 1980 (paper).
London: Fontana Lions, 1979 (paper).
Foreign editions: British, Danish, Dutch, German, Hebrew, Italian, Japanese, Portuguese, Serbo-Croatian, Swedish.

Fifth of the Prydain Chronicles. Taran, Eilonwy, and the armies of Don rally for the final battle against Arawn and the forces of evil. Taran finally discovers his destiny as the age of enchantments draws to an end.

Y17. *The Illyrian Adventure.* New York: Dutton, 1986.
New York: Dell, 1987 (paper).
Foreign editions: Danish, German, Japanese, Swedish.

First of the Vesper Holly adventures. Trying to prove her dead father's archaeological theories true, Vesper travels to Illyria where she and her guardian are endangered by a rebellion and by a ruthless rival.

Y18. *The Jedera Adventure.* New York: Dutton, 1989.

Fourth of the Vesper Holly adventures. When trying to return a book to the renowned library of Bel-Saaba in the North African country of Jedera, Vesper stumbles upon another villainous scheme of Dr. Helvitius.

Y19. *The Kestrel.* New York: Dutton, 1982.
New York: Dell, 1983 (paper).
Foreign editions: Danish, Dutch, German, Swedish.

Second of the Westmark trilogy. War breaks out in Westmark as Mickle is crowned queen. Theo becomes a fearless and feared captain known as the Kestrel. The horrors of war change him and Westmark forever.

Y20. *The King's Fountain.* New York: Dutton, 1971, 1989.
New York: Dutton, 1989 (paper).
Foreign editions: Dutch, German.

A king decides to build a fountain that would cut off the water to the city below his palace. After failed attempts to dissuade the king by others wiser and stronger, a poor man must go to the monarch himself.

Y21. *The Marvelous Misadventures of Sebastian.* New York: Dutton, 1970.
New York: Dutton, 1973 (paper).
Foreign editions: Danish, Dutch, Finnish, German, Japanese, Swedish.

Sebastian, unemployed court fiddler, wanders the kingdom getting into
one scrape after another until he rescues a princess and finds a violin
that plays music beyond his wildest dreams.

Y22. *The Philadelphia Adventure.* New York: Dutton, 1990.

Fifth of the Vesper Holly adventures. Vesper uncovers another
heinous plot of Dr. Helvitius and prevents a disaster that would have
destroyed Philadelphia's Centennial exhibition.

Y23. *The Second Chronicles of Prydain.* London: Fontana, 1986.

Includes *Taran Wanderer* and *The High King.*

Y24. *Taran Wanderer.* New York: Holt, Rinehart and Winston, 1967.
New York: Dell, 1969, 1980 (paper).
London: Fontana Lions, 1979 (paper).
Foreign editions: British, Danish, Dutch, Finnish, German, Hebrew,
Italian, Japanese, Portuguese, Swedish.

Fourth of the Prydain Chronicles. Taran quests for his parentage,
hoping it is noble so he might wed Princess Eilonwy. His search leads
him to new friends and enemies and to unexpected answers about his
identity.

Y25. *Time Cat.* New York: Holt, Rinehart and Winston, 1963.
New York: Avon, 1973, 1975 (paper).
New York: Dell, 1985 (paper).
Foreign editions: Arabic, British, German, Swedish.

Jason's cat, Gareth, has the ability to visit each of his nine lives, each of
which is in a different land and period of history. Cat and master
travel together and experience dangerous and exciting adventures.

Y26. *The Town Cats and Other Tales.* New York: Dutton, 1977.
New York: Dell, 1981 (paper).
Foreign editions: Danish, Dutch, French, German, Japanese,
Norwegian, Swedish.

Eight tales of cats, each reflecting a different style of folk tale, offer
insight and hope by revealing the folly and wisdom of humanity.

Y27. *The Truthful Harp*. New York: Holt, Rinehart and Winston, 1967.
New York: Holt Owlet, 1967 (paper).
Foreign editions: Japanese.

A Prydain picture book. Fflewddur Fflam fails the bardic exam but is
given a special harp by the Chief Bard. In his travels, Fflewddur
discovers that with each stretching of the truth, his harp breaks a string.

Y28. *Westmark*. New York: Dutton, 1981.
New York: Dell, 1982 (paper).
Foreign editions: Danish, Dutch, French, German, Swedish.

First of the Westmark trilogy. Theo, the printer's devil, violates strict
publishing laws and must flee from the authorities. Because of strange
new companions, his life is filled with adventure, intrigue, and
revolution.

Y29. *The Wizard in the Tree*. New York: Dutton, 1975.
New York: Dell, 1981 (paper).
Foreign editions: Danish, Dutch, German, Japanese, Swedish.

Mallory finds an ancient wizard locked within a tree. The innocent
wizard, whose powers are not in good working order, is accused of
murder by a villainous town squire. Mallory's quick wits save both
herself and her new friend.

c. Translations by Lloyd Alexander

T 1. Eluard, Paul. *Selected Writings of Paul Eluard*. Norfolk, Connecticut:
New Directions, 1951.

Norfolk, Connecticut: New Directions, 1975 (paper).
Published as *Uninterrupted Poetry—Selected Writings of Paul Eluard*.
Westport, Connecticut: Greenwood Press, 1977.

Survey of Eluard's entire body of poetry with important works from
each of his previous collections. Original poems on left pages with
Alexander's English translation of each on the facing right page.

T 2. "Little Anthology of French Poetry." In *New Directions in Prose and
Poetry Annual No. 10*. Ed. James Laughlin. New York: New
Directions, 1948, pp. 340-370.

Translation of a collection of poems from different French poets.

T 3. Sartre, Jean-Paul. *Nausea*. New York: New Directions, 1949.
      New York: New Directions, 1959, 1964 (paper).

      Sartre's first novel of a man expressing his confusion and despair at the
      world in which he lives. While Sartre became known through his
      other novels, *Nausea* has come to be recognized as his most enduring
      book.

T 4. Sartre, Jean-Paul. *The Wall and Other Stories*. New York: New
          Directions, 1949 (c. 1948).
      New York: Berkley, 1956 (paper). Published as *Intimacy and Other
      Stories*. London: Panther (Hamilton), 1960 (paper). Published as
      Intimacy and Other Stories.

      Collection of short stories about a variety of modern French
      personalities.

T 5. Vialar, Paul. *The Sea Rose*. London: Peter Nevill, Ltd., 1951.

      Novel which centers on an unhappy love affair.

d. Foreign editions of Lloyd Alexander's work

Arabic:

F 1. *Rihlat al Kut el Aageeb (Time Cat)*. Cairo: Halaby, 1968.

British:

F 2. *The Black Cauldron*. London: Heinemann, 1967.
F 3. *The Book of Three*. London: Heinemann, 1966.
F 4. *The Castle of Llyr*. London: Heinemann, 1968.
F 5. *The Four Donkeys*. Tadworth: World's Work, 1974.
F 6. *The High King*. London: Collins, 1979.
F 7. *Janine is French*. London: Cassell, 1960.
F 8. *My Five Tigers*. London: Cassell, 1956.
F 9. *My Love Affair with Music*. London: Cassell, 1961.
F10. *Nine Lives (Time Cat)*. London: Cassell, 1963.
F11. *Park Avenue Vet*. London: Deutsch, 1962.
F12. *Send for Ryan! (Fifty Years in the Doghouse)*. London: Allen, 1965.
F13. *Taran Wanderer*. London: Collins, 1979.

Danish:

F14. *Frihedens Klokker (Westmark)*. Copenhagen: Høst, 1983.
F15. *Hittebarnet (The Foundling)*. Copenhagen: Forum, 1985.
F16. *Katten der Sagde Nej (The Town Cats)*. Copenhagen: Forum, 1984.
F17. *Kong Taran (The High King)*. Copenhagen: Forum, 1983.

F18. *Lukas-Kashas to Første Liv* (*The First Two Lives of Lukas-Kasha*). Copenhagen: Høst, 1986.
F19. *Sebastians Saelsomme Eventyr* (*The Marvelous Misadventures of Sebastian*). Copenhagen: Forum, 1986.
F20. *Taran Vandringsmand* (*Taran Wanderer*). Copenhagen: Forum, 1982.
F21. *Tårnfalken* (*The Kestrel*). Copenhagen: Høst, 1984.
F22. *Tarans Første Rejse* (*The Book of Three*). Copenhagen: Forum, 1980.
F23. *Tarans og Borgen på Øen* (*The Castle of Llyr*). Copenhagen: Forum, 1982.
F24. *Tarans og Mørkeridderne* (*The Black Cauldron*). Copenhagen: Forum, 1981.
F25. *Tiggerdronningen* (*The Beggar Queen*). Copenhagen: Høst, 1985.
F26. *Trolmanden i Traeet* (*The Wizard in the Tree*). Copenhagen: Forum, 1987.

Dutch:

F27. *De Buitengewone Belevenissen van Sebastian* (*The Marvelous Misadventures of Sebastian*). Hoorn: West-Friesland, 1979.
F28. *Dappere Coll en Andere Verhalen* (*Coll and His White Pig, The Four Donkeys*, and *The King's Fountain*). Hoorn: West-Friesland, 1982.
F29. *The Drackenberg Adventure*. Hoorn: Facet.
F30. *The El Dorado Adventure*. Hoorn: Facet.
F31. *De Eerste Twee Levens van Lukas-Kasha* (*The First Two Lives of Lukas-Kasha*). Hoorn: West-Friesland, 1980.
F32. *De Grote Konig* (*The High King*). Hoorn: West-Friesland, 1976.
F33. *Het Boek van Drie* (*The Book of Three*). Hoorn: West-Friesland, 1973.
F34. *De Kasteel van Llyr* (*The Castle of Llyr*). Hoorn: West-Friesland, 1975.
F35. *De Kat die een Mens Wilde Zijn* (*The Cat Who Wished to be a Man*). Hoorn: West-Friesland, 1978.
F36. *The Kestrel*. Hoorn: West-Friesland.
F37. *Mijn Kleine Tijgers* (*My Five Tigers*). Hoorn: West-Friesland, 1983.
F38. *De Straatkatten* (*The Town Cats*). Hoorn: West-Friesland, 1979.
F39. *Taran Zwerver* (*Taran Wanderer*). Hoorn: West-Friesland, 1975.
F40. *De Tovennar in de Boom* (*The Wizard in the Tree*). Hoorn: West-Friesland, 1975.
F41. *De Vondeling* (*The Foundling*). Hoorn: West-Friesland, 1976.
F42. *Westmark* (*Westmark*). Hoorn: West-Friesland, 1982.
F43. *De Zwarte Ketel* (*The Black Cauldron*). Hoorn: West-Friesland, 1974.

Finnish:

F44. *Hiidenpata* (*The Black Cauldron*). Helsinki: Gummerus/Weilin & Göös, 1989.
F45. *Llyrin Linna* (*The Castle of Llyr*). Helsinki: Gummerus/Weilin & Göös, 1989.
F46. *Kolmen Kertomus* (*The Book of Three*). Helsinki: Weilin & Göös, 1987.

F47. *The Marvelous Misadventures of Sebastian*. Helsinki: Weilin & Göös.
F48. *Taran Wanderer*. Helsinki: Weilin & Göös.

French:

F49. *Le Chaudron Noir* (*The Black Cauldron*). Paris: Livre de Poche, 1985.
F50. *Le Livre des Trois* (*The Book of Three*). Paris: Livre de Poche, 1985.
F51. *La Princesse et le Charlatan* (*Westmark*). Paris: Livre de Poche, 1986.
F52. *La Ville des Chats* (*The Town Cats*). Paris: Livre de Poche, 1983.

German:

F53. *Abenteuer in Illyrien* (*The Illyrian Adventure*). Stuttgart/Vienna: Thienemann, 1988.
F54. *Der Arme Mann und der König* (*The King's Fountain*). Vienna: St. Gabriel, 1984.
F55. *Aufruhr in Westmark* (*Westmark*). Würzburg: Arena, 1983.
F56. *Die Bettler Königin* (*The Beggar Queen*). Würzburg: Arena, 1985.
F57. *Das El Dorado Abenteuer* (*The El Dorado Adventure*). Stuttgart/ Vienna: Thienemann, 1988.
F58. *Janine Meine Frau, die Französin* (*Janine is French*). Tübingen: Wunderlich, 1961.
F59. *Lukas Kasha oder der Trick des Gauklers* (*The First Two Lives of Lukas-Kasha*). Stuttgart: Boje, 1983.
F60. *Mallory und der Zauberer im Baum* (*The Wizard in the Tree*). Erlangen: Boje, 1985.
F61. *Ein Mann und Tausend Tiere* (*Fifty Years in the Doghouse*). Rüschlikon-Zürich: Müller, 1967.
F62. *Musik, Meine Launische Geliebte* (*My Love Affair with Music*). Tübingen: Wunderlich, 1963.
F63. *Die Nächste Katze Bitte* (*Park Avenue Vet*). Tübingen: Wunderlich, 1965.
F64. *Sebastians Wundersame Abenteuer* (*The Marvelous Misadventures of Sebastian*). Erlangen: Boje, 1986.
F65. *Die Stadtkatzen* (*The Town Cats*). Stuttgart: Boje, 1983.
F66. *Taran und das Zauberschwein* (*The Book of Three*). Würzburg: Arena, 1969.
F67. *Taran und das Zauberschwert* (*The High King*). Würzburg: Arena, 1974.
F68. *Taran und der Zauberkatze* (*The Castle of Llyr*). Würzburg: Arena, 1972.
F69. *Taran und der Zauberkessel* (*The Black Cauldron*). Würzburg: Arena, 1970.
F70. *Taran und der Zauberspiegel* (*Taran Wanderer*). Würzburg: Arena, 1972.
F71. *Der Turmfalke* (*The Kestrel*). Würzburg: Arena, 1984.
F72. *Vom Katzchen, das ein Mensch Sein Wollte* (*The Cat Who Wished to be a Man*). Stuttgart: Boje, 1984.

F73.   *Die Zietkatze (Time Cat)*. Würzburg: Arena, 1986.

Hebrew:

F74.   *The Black Cauldron*. Tel Aviv: Zmora Bitan, 1986.
F75.   *The Book of Three*. Tel Aviv: Zmora Bitan.
F76.   *The Castle of Llyr*. Tel Aviv: Zmora Bitan.
F77.   *Hamelech Haelyon (The High King)*. Tel Aviv: Zmora Bitan, 1986.
F78.   *Shtay Parshiyot Chayav Harishonot Shel Lukas-Kasha (The First Two Lives of Lukas-Kasha)*. Tel Aviv: Zmora Bitan, 1987.
F79.   *Taran Wanderer*. Tel Aviv: Zmora Bitan.

Italian:

F80.   *Il Calderone Nero (The Black Cauldron)*. Verona: Mondadori, 1986.
F81.   *La Saga di Prydain (The Book of Three, The Black Cauldron, and The Castle of Llyr* in one volume). Milan: Editrice Nord, 1986.

Japanese:

F82.   *The Black Cauldron*. Tokyo: Hyoron-Sha, 1974.
F83.   *The Book of Three*. Tokyo: Hyoron-Sha, 1974.
F84.   *The Castle of Llyr*. Tokyo: Hyoron-Sha, 1974.
F85.   *The Cat Who Wished to be a Man*. Tokyo: Hyoron-Sha, 1977.
F86.   *Coll and His White Pig*. Tokyo: Hyoron-Sha, 1980.
F87.   *The El Dorado Adventure*. Tokyo: Hyoron-Sha.
F88.   *The High King*. Tokyo: Hyoron-Sha, 1977.
F89.   *The Illyrian Adventure*. Tokyo: Hyoron-Sha.
F90.   *The Marvelous Misadventures of Sebastian*. Tokyo: Hyoron-Sha, 1977.
F91.   *Taran Wanderer*. Tokyo: Hyoron-Sha, 1976.
F92.   *The Town Cats*. Tokyo: Hyoron-Sha, 1988.
F93.   *The Truthful Harp*. Tokyo: Hyoron-Sha, 1980.
F94.   *The Wizard in the Tree*. Tokyo: Hyoron-Sha, 1977.

Norwegian:

F95.   *Katten Som Sa Nei (The Town Cats)*. Oslo: Tiden Norsk, 1986.
F96.   *Lukas-Kasha Hans To Første Liv (The First Two Lives of Lukas-Kasha)*. Oslo: Tiden Norsk, 1980.
F97.   *Taran og den Magiske Grisen (The Book of Three)*. Oslo: Tiden Norsk, 1981.
F98.   *Taran og Slottet Llyr (The Castle of Llyr)*. Oslo: Tiden Norsk, 1984.
F99.   *Taran og den Sorte Gryte (The Black Cauldron)*. Oslo: Tiden Norsk, 1982.

Portuguese:

F100. *O Caldeirão Mágico (The Black Cauldron)*. Lisbon: Europa-America, 1987.

F101. *O Castelo de Llyr* (*The Castle of Llyr*). Lisbon: Europa-America, 1987.
F102. *O Errante Taran* (*Taran Wanderer*). Lisbon: Europa-America, 1987.
F103. *O Grande Rei* (*The High King*). Lisbon: Europa-America, 1987.
F104. *O Livro de Três* (*The Book of Three*). Lisbon: Europa-America, 1987.

Serbo-Croatian:

F105. *The High King*. Gornji Milanovac: Decjne Novine.

Spanish:

F106. *El Caldero Mágico* (*The Black Cauldron*). Barcelona: Martinez-Roca, 1988.
F107. *El Libro de los Tres* (*The Book of Three*). Barcelona: Martinez-Roca, 1987.

Swedish:

F108. *Äventyr i Drackenberg* (*The Drackenberg Adventure*). Stockholm: Sjöstrands, 1988.
F109. *Äventyr i El Dorado* (*The El Dorado Adventure*). Stockholm: Sjöstrands, 1987.
F110. *Äventyr i Illyrien* (*The Illyrian Adventure*). Stockholm: Sjöstrands, 1986.
F111. *Hittebarnet* (*The Foundling*). Stockholm: Sjöstrands, 1983.
F112. *Katten Som Sa Nej* (*The Town Cats*). Stockholm: Sjöstrands, 1979.
F113. *Katten Som Ville bli Människa* (*The Cat Who Wished to be a Man*). Stockholm: Sjöstrands, 1985.
F114. *Llyrs Slott* (*The Castle of Llyr*). Stockholm: Sjöstrands, 1982.
F115. *Lukas-Kashas Två Första Liv* (*The First Two Lives of Lukas-Kasha*). Stockholm: Sjöstrands, 1982.
F116. *Mina Fem Tigrar* (*My Five Tigers*). Stockholm: Sjöstrands, 1984.
F117. *Sebastians Underbara Missöden och Äventyr* (*The Marvelous Misadventures of Sebastian*). Stockholm: Sjöstrands, 1980.
F118. *Storkonungen* (*The High King*). Stockholm: Berghs, 1973. (Stockholm: Sjöstrands, 1984.)
F119. *Den Svarta Kitteln* (*The Black Cauldron*). Stockholm: Sjöstrands, 1981.
F120. *Taran Vandraren* (*Taran Wanderer*). Stockholm: Sjöstrands, 1983.
F121. *Tidskatten* (*Time Cat*). Stockholm: Sjöstrands, 1983.
F122. *Tiggardrottningen* (*The Beggar Queen*). Stockholm: Sjöstrands, 1984.
F123. *Tornfalken* (*The Kestrel*). Stockholm: Sjöstrands, 1983.
F124. *De Trennes Bok* (*The Book of Three*). Stockholm: Sjöstrands, 1981.
F125. *Trollkarlen i Trädet* (*The Wizard in the Tree*). Stockholm: Sjöstrands, 1982.
F126. *Väster om Friheten* (*Westmark*). Stockholm: Sjöstrands, 1982.

2. Shorter Fiction by Lloyd Alexander

S 1.   "Cuisine Janine." *Philadelphia Bulletin*, 17 September 1961, p. 17.

Interview with Janine and Lloyd, focusing upon the aspect of French war bride and struggling writer making a life together. Included is Janine's favorite recipe.

S 2.   "The Cat and the Golden Egg." In *Wind by the Sea*. Ed. P. David Pearson et al. Needham, Massachusetts: Silver Burdett and Ginn, 1989, pp. 263-274. (from *The Town Cats*.)

When the cupboards are bare in his mistress' house, her clever cat turns the tables on the crooked grocer and fills them at the swindler's expense.

S 3.   "The Cat-King's Daughter." In *Beacons* (Level M). Ed. William K. Durr et al. Boston: Houghton Mifflin, 1981, pp. 333-346. (from *The Town Cats*.)

The capricious king forbids his daughter to marry the prince of her choice. Only when her cat intervenes is all made right between the lovers and in the kingdom as a whole.

S 4.   "Dorothea." In *Discovery No. 3*. Ed. Vance Bourjaily. New York: Pocketbooks, 1954, pp. 27-37.

A young man on his first job meets an enticing girl who lives with her wealthy and controlling mother. The couple shares a bittersweet relationship which ends when the girl defies her mother and is sent away to college.

S 5.   "Dream-of-Jade: The Emperor's Cat (How Dream-of-Jade Looked at the Emperor)." *Cricket*, 4 (October 1976): 12-19.

No one is to look at the Celestial Emperor, Kwan-Yu. Dream-of-Jade, a green-eyed cat, does not lower her eyes and while examining the Emperor notices loose ceiling tiles about to fall upon the holy ruler.

S 6.   "Dream-of-Jade: The Emperor's Cat (How Dream-of-Jade Cured the Emperor)." *Cricket*, 4 (November 1976): 13-20.

Dream-of-Jade, the Emperor's cat, watches three medical charlatans offer cures to her listless master. She later tricks the Emperor into some hard work, which restores appetite and sound sleep.

S 7.   "Dream-of-Jade: The Emperor's Cat (How Dream-of-Jade Wrote the
       Law)." *Cricket*, 4 (December 1976): 14-20.

       Dream-of-Jade, the Celestial Emperor's wise cat, exposes the Chief
       Minister as an inept blowhard who has written laws that make no
       sense. Dream-of-Jade becomes Chief Minister and writes the Emperor's
       laws.

S 8.   "The Fantastic Symphony." In *New Directions in Prose and Poetry
       Annual No. 11*. Ed. James Laughlin. New York: New Directions,
       1949, pp. 47-59.

       Fashioned after the form of Berlioz's "Fantastic Symphony," this 13
       page stream of consciousness work is written in five parts, as is the
       original musical score it imitates, each introduced by Berlioz' own
       notes on the composition.

S 9.   "Fifty Years in the Monkey House and Other Hangouts of the ASPCA
       Special Agents." *McCall's*, 91 (February 1964):110-111+.

       A brief look at the ASPCA through some of the unusual situations and
       anecdotes experienced by its Special Agent No. 1, William Michael
       Ryan.

S10.   "The Foundling." In *The Fantastic Imagination*. Ed. Robert H. Boyer
       and Kenneth J. Zahorski. New York: Avon, 1977. (from *The
       Foundling and Other Tales of Prydain*.)

       Dallben is found and raised by the witches Orddu, Orwen, and Orgoch.
       When he accidentally tastes a brew of wisdom, he is asked to leave.
       Dallben is allowed to choose a parting gift; he takes *The Book of Three*.

S11.   "Heathcliff." In *Best Cat Stories*. Ed. Leslie O'Mara. London: O'Mara
       Books Limited, 1989, pp. 194-206. (from *My Five Tigers*.)

       The second of Alexander's original five tigers, Heathcliff was named
       because of his similarity to Emily Brontë's handsome and morose
       character and lived up to his dramatic name.

S12.   "The Highest Bid." *Cricket*, 17 (September 1989): 37-41. (excerpt from
       The Jedera Adventure.)

       Vesper and Brinnie are auctioned as slaves in the African country of
       Jedera. A mysterious, fearsome stranger purchases them for one
       copper coin, for no one dares bid against him.

S13.   "The Highest Bid, Part 2." *Cricket*, 17 (October 1989): 72-76. (excerpt from *The Jedera Adventure*.)

Vesper and Brinnie are freed by the mysterious stranger who bought them at a slave auction and discover him to be a friend. They are then able to continue their journey, accompanied by the French Foreign Legion.

S14.   "The House Gobaleen." In an anthology of fantasy stories. Ed. by Jean Greenlaw. Forthcoming.

With the flavor of an Irish fairy tale, this humorous short story centers upon a greedy and disagreeable goblin who takes up residence with a farmer and his cat. The cat very cleverly manages to root the goblin out of the house.

S15.   "How the Cat Swallowed Thunder." *Just for Fun*. Ed. Ann Durell. New York: Dutton, 1977, pp. 3-12.

A disobedient cat breaks the rules when his mistress is away, and the result is the tiny thundering in cats which registers their approval and contentedness.

S16.   "Miklan Tells a Tale: The Pearls and the Pie." *Cricket*, 2 (May 1975): 11-15.

Miklan, a street urchin and trickster, bargains with a local baker to trade a story for a piece of freshly baked plum pie.

S17.   "The Pearls and the Pie: Miklan Ends a Tale." *Cricket*, 2 (June 1975): 11-15.

Miklan, tricking his "host" into providing food and drink, finishes telling the story about a young baker and a princess who are married when the princess' lost necklace is discovered in one of the baker's plum pies.

S18.   "My Friend Rembrandt, Part I." *World Over*, 23 (5 January 1962), pp. 12-13.

Ephraim Hezekiah Bueno, a Jewish doctor in Amsterdam, tells the story of having his portrait painted by Rembrandt van Rijn.

S19.   "My Friend Rembrandt, Part II." *World Over*, 23 (19 January 1962), pp. 12-13.

Ephraim Bueno is summoned to the bedside of Rembrandt's ailing wife, who eventually dies. But during the weeks of treatment, Bueno learns much about the painter and his affinity for the Jewish people.

S20. "My Friend Rembrandt, Part III." *World Over*, 23 (2 February 1962), pp. 12-13.

Bueno recounts Rembrandt's inability to paint after his wife's death, his eventual return to painting, his decline in popularity, his remarriage, and, finally, his financial ruin.

S21. "My Friend Rembrandt, Part IV." *World Over*, 23 (16 February 1962), pp. 12-13.

Rembrandt disappears, and Bueno does not see him for many months. Living as a pauper, Rembrandt paints Biblical scenes using poor Jews as models instead of portraits of the rich. He paints only to please himself.

S22. "The Phoenix, Part I." *World Over*, 26 (9 October 1964), pp. 12-13.

David Israel writes his story for the benefit of his new grandson. He had lived in the Dutch colonies in Brazil, where Jews escaped the Inquisition. One evening he and a friend spot Portuguese soldiers ready to invade.

S23. "The Phoenix, Part II." *World Over*, 26 (23 October 1964), pp. 12-13.

David Israel joins a Dutch unit that defends the Brazilian colonies from the Portuguese, who are raiding settlements and killing Jews. In a battle, David's unit is captured by the cold-hearted General Vidal.

S24. "The Phoenix, Part III." *World Over*, 26 (6 November 1964), pp. 12-13.

A part of David Israel's unit is rescued from the Portuguese, but David is wounded in a later skirmish. After his recovery, David and the town of Recife are beseiged for six months in what becomes a war of starvation.

S25. "The Phoenix, Part IV." *World Over*, 26 (20 November 1964), pp. 12-13.

David and the town of Recife are saved by Dutch ships that run the Portuguese blockade. Years later the Portuguese mount a strong attack, and the Dutch colonies crumble. The Jews of Brazil are allowed to emigrate.

S26. "The Smith, the Weaver, and the Harper."   In *The Fantastic Imagination II*. Ed. Robert H. Boyer and Kenneth J. Zahorski. New York: Avon, 1978.

"The Smith, the Weaver, and the Harper." In *The Newbery Reader*. Ed. Charles G. Waugh and Martin H. Greenberg. New York: Harcourt, 1984, pp. 1-9. (from *The Foundling and Other Tales of Prydain*.)

Arawn tricks the craftsmen of Prydain into trading away their enchanted tools. However, he cannot trick the bard, Menwy, who sees through the Death-Lord's ruse and preserves his wonderful harp and its musical secrets.

S27. "The Stone." *Cricket*, 1 (October 1973): 60-69. (from *The Foundling and Other Tales of Prydain*.)

The cottager Maibon frees Doli of the Fair Folk from a fallen log and demands a wish be granted, that of never aging. The wish becomes a curse from which Maibon cannot escape until he truly desires a normal life.

S28. "The Sword." In *The Year's Best Fantasy Stories*. Ed. by Lin Carter. New York: Daw Books, 1975. (from *The Foundling and Other Tales of Prydain*.)

King Rhitta uses the sword Dyrnwyn to slay the shepherd Amyrs, whose blood permanently stains the blade black. Trying in vain to hide from his guilt in a maze of passages below Spiral Castle, Rhitta meets his doom.

S29. "The Three Talking Horses." *Cricket*, 6 (June 1979): 38-43. (excerpt from *The First Two Lives of Lukas-Kasha*.)

Lukas tricks the horse trader, Katir, into returning Nur-Jehan's stolen and much beloved white stallion. His ruse convinces Katir that his horses can speak and know where treasure is hidden.

S30. "The True Enchanter." *Cricket*, 1 (November 1973): 32-42.
Reprinted in *Cricket*, 15 (December 1987): 49-56. "The True Enchanter." In *Emblems* (Level N). Ed. William K. Durr et al. Boston: Houghton Mifflin, 1981, pp. 191-201. (from *The Foundling and Other Tales of Prydain*.)
"Le Vrai Magicien." *Astrapi* (1 June 1989), p. 9-11. ("The True Enchanter," published in a French children's magazine.)

Princess Angharad must wed an enchanter but is not impressed with any of her powerful suitors. Instead, she makes the unpopular choice of Geraint, a young man who weaves enchantments through storytelling.

S31. "Twenty Thousand Cats in My Life." *McCall's*, 89 (July 1962): 72-73+.

Experiences of Dr. Louis J. Camuti, who spent most of his career as a
veterinarian treating only cats in New York City.

S32. "The Two Brothers." Illustrated by Dirk Zimmer. *The Big Book for
Peace.* New York: Dutton, 1989.

Two headstrong and stubborn brothers manage to ruin each other
through sheer stupidity in this comic tale.

3. Other Writings by Lloyd Alexander

W 1. Acceptance speech for the Regina Medal of the Catholic Library
Association. *Catholic Library World*, 58 (July/August 1986): 14-15.

Alexander recounts his early and unsuccessful writing endeavors and
then explains that a writer must discover that the work does not serve
his purpose—his "purpose is to serve the work."

W 2. "The Alchemical Experience." *Library News Bulletin*, 37 (January
1970): 28-29.

Fantasy concerns itself with reality and with the human being. While
differences exist between realistic fiction and fantasy, the similarities
are far more important for both literature and the reader. The role of
each to is help us make better choices and become better people.

W 3. "The American Book Award Acceptance." *Horn Book*, 58 (October
1982): 571.

Alexander accepts "very happily a very great honor," the American
Book Award for hardcover children's fiction for *Westmark*. He states
that the perplexities found in the country of Westmark are the same as
the ones we face in our lives.

W 4. "Bad Ankle, Cold Feet." *YA People* (Children's Book Council), 1, No. 1
(1989).

Alexander's short response to a query for his most embarrassing
moment, which was a badly sprained ankle just hours before his first
date—an evening at the big high school dance. Because he had been so
hesitant about the evening, no one believed his story and the girl
never talked to him again.

W 5. "Books Remembered." *The Calendar* (Children's Book Council), (March-October, 1981).

Alexander explains why his most important childhood book was a 30 pound dictionary. Leading the reader on a personal tour of its pages, he reveals to the reader boyhood memories surrounding the book itself and some of the memorabilia he has stuck between its pages.

W 6. "Cricket's Bookshelf." Rev. of *Babar* (Random House), by Jean de Brunhoff, *Cricket*, 1 (February 1974): 94-95.

Alexander presents an overview of the Babar series, mentioning why he likes the elephant and other characters in the books.

W 7. "Cricket's Bookshelf." Rev. of *Just So Stories* (Doubleday), by Rudyard Kipling, *Cricket*, 1 (April 1974): 94-95.

Introduction of Kipling's stories to young readers, with emphases on the make-believe, the magical words, and the appeal of hearing these tales read aloud.

W 8. "Cricket's Bookshelf." Rev. of *Prayers from the Ark* (French and European Publications, Inc.), by Carmen Bernos de Gasztold, *Cricket*, 2 (November 1974): 94-95.

This poetry by Carmen Bernos de Gasztold is a collection of short and heartfelt prayers offered by animals. From the poems we can see that some of the things which concern animals are also of concern to us.

W 9. "Fantasy and the Human Condition." *The New Advocate*, 1 (Spring 1988): 75-83.

Alexander proposes that fantasy and realism are not opposites but "two modes of expressing the same thing." "Ultimately, fantasy depends not on cleverness, but on human truth."

W10. "Fantasy as Images: A Literary View." *Language Arts*, 55 (April 1978): 440-446.

Alexander defends the arts and fantasy literature as a part of the arts. He discusses the deep, emotional imagery of fantasy, its psychological and educational validity, its societal influence, and its "playfulness"— one of the most creative of human qualities.

W11. "The Flat-heeled Muse." *Horn Book*, 41 (April 1965): 141-146.
Reprinted in *Children and Literature: Views and Reviews*. Ed. Virginia Haviland. Glenview, Illinois: Scott, Foresman, 1965, pp. 241-245.

Largely through a conversation between author and muse in charge of fantasy, Alexander shows how good fantasy is based in logic and reality, not whim and unfettered imagination. A sharp and focused look at what makes good fantasy.

W12. Foreword. *Fantasy Literature: A Core Collection and Reference Guide*. Ed. Marshall B. Tymn, Kenneth J. Zahorski, and Robert H. Boyer. New York: R.R. Bowker, 1979, p. 40-44.

Alexander builds a case for fantasy literature being useful though perhaps not utilitarian. He examines its ability to provide hope, foster imagination, and move us deeply at levels "not often accessible through works of surface realism." "What metaphor is to language, fantasy is to literature."

W13. Foreword. *Introducing Books: A Guide for the Middle Grades*. By John Gillespie and Diana Lembo. New York: R.R. Bowker, 1970, pp. xi-xiv.

Recounting his own experience as a young reader, Alexander focuses attention for adult users of this anthology away from formal presentations of books toward the natural involvement and sharing of interesting titles.

W14. Foreword. *The Prydain Companion: A Reference Guide to Alexander's Chronicles of Prydain*. By Michael O. Tunnell. New York: Greenwood Press, 1989.

In an introduction to this work, Alexander explains how *The Prydain Companion* might be helpful to prospective readers, both fans of his Prydain books and those who have not read them.

W15. "A Gift from Gertrude Stein." *Cricket*, 4 (January 1977): 54-59.

While living in Paris in 1945, Lloyd Alexander visited the famous American author, Gertrude Stein. He tells how this awe-inspiring creative genius encouraged a young writer-to-be and gives some background information about this unusual woman.

W16. "The Grammar of Story." In *Celebrating Children's Books*. Ed. Betsy Hearne and Marilyn Kaye. New York: Lothrop, 1981, pp. 3-13.

Story "convinces us of its reality" by creating believable illusions. Certain elements in writing help to structure these illusions, and Alexander examines them using the metaphor of grammar to explain how stories work.

W17. "High Fantasy and Heroic Romance." *Horn Book*, 47 (December 1971): 577-584.

In this era of science and reality, connections with the past—specifically the age-old mythologies and stories—can bring understanding to those living in the modern world.

W18. "How Does the Author View His Relationship to His Audience?" *Elementary English*, 45 (November 1968): 932-933.

The author has a responsibility to the audience to give it the best possible book, and that is not possible without respect for the reader. Writing a book is not self-indulgence. "The writer who functions as both creator and craftsman not only serves his readers, he serves his own art."

W19. "A Hungry Reader." (With illustrations by Lloyd Alexander.) *Cricket*, 1 (January 1973): 74-76.
Reprinted in *Cricket*, 16 (April 1989): 34-35.

When he was young, Alexander liked to eat while he read—but he preferred food from the book. While reading *Treasure Island*, for instance, he ate an apple just as Jim Hawkins did. But Lloyd couldn't find venison and ale to join Robin Hood, so a hamburger and root beer had to do.

W20. "Identifications and Identities." *Wilson Library Bulletin*, 45 (October 1970): 144-148.

Reading a good book is a pleasure, but it is also a means of identifying who we are and who we are becoming. The situations and characters in books help us to learn about and understand ourselves.

W21. Introduction. *The Dark Frigate*. By Charles Boardman Hawes. New York: Little, Brown & Co., 1970, pp. ix-xiii.

The Dark Frigate is more than an adventure. In its pages are unforgettable characters, truths about life and its difficulties, and a modernity unexpected in a book published in the 1920s.

W22. Letter. "Lloyd Alexander." In *A Treasury of Letters from Favorite Authors Book Two*. By Nancy Polette. O'Fallon, Missouri: Book Lures, 1979, p. 3.

A brief handwritten letter from Lloyd Alexander to his young readers appears in this collection of letters from authors. He talks of his love for reading as a youngster and explains that writers are real people who are most fulfilled when their books become part of a reader's life.

W23. "Letter to the Editor." *Orcrist*, 4 (16 January 1969): 10.

Alexander's letter acknowledges the editor's accuracy in showing parallels between Prydain and the *Mabinogion* and includes some additional details not mentioned.

W24. "Literature, Creativity and Imagination." *Childhood Education*, 47 (March 1971): 307-310.

Reprinted in *Association for Childhood Education International*. Ed. Patricia Maloney Markun. Washington, D.C.: Association for Childhood Education International, 1973, pp. 3-6.

Before adults can help children see the power of growth and learning from literature, they must experience it themselves. The reader is an active part of the creative process in literature.

W25. "Meet Your Author." *Cricket*, 4 (December 1976): 22.

Brief autobiographical look at Alexander's desire to be a writer and how he can get his ideas without leaving home by using his imagination.

W26. "A Manner of Speaking." In *The Voice of the Narrator in Children's Literature*. Ed. Charlotte F. Otten and Gary D. Schmidt. New York: Greenwood, 1989, pp. 123-131.

Alexander discusses the narrative "voice" of the storyteller and decides that "we can have tone and style without voice, but not voice without style and tone." He then examines the fantasy genre to determine if it has its own particular tone, style, and voice. He considers his own work.

W27. "Meet Your Author: Lloyd Alexander (Who Wrote Dream-of-Jade)." *Cricket*, 4 (December 1976): 22.

Addressing his young fans, Alexander tells about using his imagination to conjure story ideas, suggesting that using one's imagination will always create "the brightest adventures."

W28. "Newbery Award Acceptance." *Horn Book*, 45 (August 1969): 378-381.

Alexander speaks of his uncertainties as a writer, reminisces about the meaning of Prydain in his life, ponders the power of art in the human life, and ends with the idea that we are to give children hope.

W29. "No Laughter in Heaven." *Horn Book*, 46 (February 1970): 11-19.

Recounting his discovery of the power of humor, Alexander makes a case for the ability humor has to instruct and clarify in both literature and life. Far from mere frivolity, "[t]he most effective, satisfying humor draws greater strength as it goes deeper to the core of the human condition; hoping to find meaning, or if finding none, hoping to create meaning."

W30. "Note on Arthurian legend." In *The Once and Future Arthur*. Ed. Ed Meskys. Center Harbor, New Hampshire: Niekas Publications, 1989, p. 35.

Alexander writes of his childhood fantasies that incorporated the stories of King Arthur. Later, he learned "that King Arthur was more than a collection of bright adventures" but "one of our profoundest mythologies"—"one of our profoundest truths."

W31. "Notes on 'The Westmark Trilogy.'" *The Advocate*, 4 (Fall 1984): 1-6.

Lloyd Alexander recounts the events that led to his beginning the Westmark series and gives a blow-by-blow account of his struggles to bring the award-winning trilogy to fruition.

W32. "Novel Ideas." *The Reading Loft Newsletter*, 1, (December 1988), pp. 8-9.

Alexander recounts the development of Vesper Holly and Professor Brinton Garrett, along with their fast-paced adventures, as an antidote to the seriousness of the Westmark trilogy which he had just finished.

W33. "Occupational Hazards." *The Advocate*, 5 (Fall 1985): 4-8.

Alexander suggests that writing is an art, not a science, and technical knowledge can only help to a limited extent, thus making it (and all the arts) a hazardous occupation. He continues to defend the arts as worthy of emphasis in public schools. ". . . the arts are what humanize us."

W34. "On Responsibility and Authority." *Horn Book*, 50 (August 1974): 363-364.
Reprinted in *Michigan Librarian*, 41 (Summer 1974), pp. 363-364.
Reprinted in *Nebraska Library Association Quarterly*, 5 (Fall 1974), pp. 9-17.

Voicing his concern about censorship, Alexander points out that "if we are to be responsible adults, we must have an equal measure of authority over our own lives." When others assume the authority, little has been done to protect our morals. "By making it impossible for us to choose *not* to read a given book or see a given film, it becomes impossible for us to be moral."

W35. "Outlooks and Insights." In *Reaching Children and Young People Through Literature.* Ed. Helen W. Painter. Newark, Delaware: International Reading Association, 1971, pp. 19-29.

This personal essay encapsulates Alexander's views on helping others to learn and become educated: everything must begin with the teacher, whose responsibility it is to be open, interested, and humane. Our vision must not be narrow. "What concerns me is this tendency to think in terms of either/or—which can lead to impoverishment, instead of both/and—which can lead to enrichment." To make a difference, we must be passionate and compassionate human beings.

W36. "The Perilous Realms: A Colloquy." In *Innocence and Experience.* Ed. Barbara Harrison and Gregory Maguire. New York: Lothrop, Lee and Shepard, 1987, pp. 195-197.

In an opening statement preceding a panel discussion, Alexander addresses the perils facing authors and literature in this age. He specifically discusses the perils to fantasy writers and to writers of realism. He then participates in a colloquy with other authors, discussing the writing of fantasy.

W37. "A Personal Note by Lloyd Alexander on Charles Dickens." *Top of the News,* 25 (November 1968): 10-14.

Alexander read Dickens again and again as a youth and continues as an adult to find insight and pleasure in his books. While Dickens is sometimes accused of having caricatures instead of characters, Alexander challenges the detractors to draw so convincing a human portrait. Dickens is important and relevant today, and "will be relevant as long as the human condition is able to move us, as long as we are still able to weep—and laugh."

W38. "A Second Look: *Five Children and It." Horn Book,* 61 (May/June 1985): 354-355.

A personal view of E. Nesbit's book about the Psammead, the grumpy Sand-fairy who is an interesting and compelling character. Alexander also includes information about the author, pointing out her strengths and the timeless appeal of this volume.

W39. "Seeing with the Third Eye." *English Journal,* 63 (May 1974): 35-50.

A teacher can offer no vision without first possessing it. Alexander gently presents the necessity for teachers to have imagination, realize change begins first with us, avoid narrow views, pay attention to the beauty of language, and accept the reality that good living and good teaching have to be done "the hard way, bit by bit."

W40. "Sex, Violence, Passion, Misery and Other Literary Pleasures." *The Advocate*, 1 (Winter 1982): 65-70.

Alexander looks at elements in art labeled negative and asks what is acceptable and what is unacceptable. Being cautious about easy answers, he suggests the acceptable should "deeply and permanently change the characters involved." While the answers are not easy, the only way to make progress is to "rely on our own inner resources."

W41. "Shoptalk with Lloyd Alexander." *Owlet Among the Colophons*, 2, Issue 3 (1967).

The author of Prydain explains the names in the series are genuinely Welsh but insists "[s]ince Prydain isn't quite Wales, the pronunciations don't have to be quite Welsh." Nevertheless, he offers background on Welsh pronunciation with rules and examples.

W42. "Starting All Over." In *Creative Writing for People Who Can't Not Write*. By Kathryn Lindskoog. Grand Rapids, Michigan: Academie/Zondervan, 1989, pp. 189-190.

Alexander states that writing should get more difficult because that means one is stretching his limits. He no longer fears, but expects, constant rewritings. With each new book it is as if "I've never written anything else before. . . . Writing, for me, is always starting all over again."

W43. "Substance and Fantasy." *Library Journal*, 91 (15 December 1966): 6157-6159.

Alexander discusses Prydain and defends fantasy as having real power in the real world. "The fantasy realm, which always makes sense, helps us understand our own realm—which seldom does."

W44. "Travel Notes." In *Innocence and Experience*. Ed. Barbara Harrison and Gregory Maguire. New York: Lothrop, Lee and Shepard, 1987, pp. 59-65.

Alexander explains that the journey of life provides the essential material for an author's creative efforts. He shows how mythology and fantasy, as well as realism, rely upon the writer's ability to draw from his own life experiences—"write what you know," but discover what it is that you do know.

W45. "Truth about Fantasy." *Top of the News*, 24 (January 1968): 168-174.

Fantasy reflects reality and truth. While it may be wondrous, "fantasy always brings us back to our own world and to ourselves." It also offers possibilities for improvement, telling us "in its own way that we're considerably more than we think we are."

W46. Untitled article for the International Round Table on World Peace. *Detskaya Literatura*, Moscow, Soviet Union, October 1986.

Many authors from around the world contributed to this issue, including Alexander, with their own statements about the need to emphasize our similarities instead of our differences and the necessity of recognizing each other as human beings in our continuing efforts to assure world peace.

W47. "Where the Novel Went." *Saturday Review*, 52 (22 March 1969): 62.

The novel is alive and well in children's literature, but books for adults are suffering.   "But the sorry state of the adult novel has come about more through the lack of talent in its individual practitioners than anything limiting in the form itself."

W48. "Wishful Thinking—Or Hopeful Dreaming."   *Horn Book*, 44 (August 1968): 382-390.
Reprinted in *Bookbird*, 7, no. 3 (1969), pp. 3-9.
"Wünsche and Träume: Phantasie in Zeitalter der Technik." *Jugend und Buch*, 18 (March 1969), pp. 5-11. ("Wishful Thinking—Or Hopeful Dreaming," published in a German journal.)

Listing and explaining reasons why fantasy has power to affect lives for good, Alexander's central argument lies in the title.   "Wishful thinking, at no matter what age we do it, is basically passive, withdrawn, isolated. It implies no effort beyond the wish itself. . . . Hopeful dreaming is an active process. The hopeful dreamer is willing to take his tumbles with the world, not insisting on the immediate gratification typical of infantile demands, but with the patience that is one sign of growing up. The hopeful dreamer says, 'If not now, maybe someday. . . .'"

4. Illustrations by Lloyd Alexander

I 1.   In "A Boy named Mary Jane." By William Cole. *Cricket*, 1 (January 1974), pp. 33-37.

I 2.   In "The Hungry Reader." *Cricket*, 1 (January 1973): 74-76.

Reprinted in *Cricket*, 16 (April 1989): 34-35.

I 3.   In "An Interview with Lloyd Alexander." By Michael O. Tunnell. *The New Advocate*, 2 (Spring 1989): 83-95.

I 4.   In "Sex, Violence, Passion, Misery and Other Literary Pleasures." *The Advocate*, 1 (Winter 1982): 65-70.

5. Unpublished Speeches and Writings of Lloyd Alexander

U 1. Acceptance speech for the Golden Cat Award. Typescript, speech presented in Stockholm, Sweden, 24 October 1984.

U 2. Acceptance speech for the Helen Keating Ott Award. Typescript, speech presented to the Church and Synagogue Library Association, Haverford, Pennsylvania, 28 June 1987.

U 3. Acceptance speech for the Carolyn W. Field Award. Typescript, speech presented in absentia to the Pennsylvania Library Association, Erie, Pennsylvania, 5 October 1987.

U 4. "The Ecology of the Imagination." Photocopy, speech presented at Third Annual Conference of Children's Literature, University of Georgia, Athens, Georgia, 7 May 1971.

U 5. "Famous Words Revisited." Typescript, speech presented at the Everychild Conference, New York City, New York, 30 August 1983.

U 6. "Future Conditional." Typescript, speech presented to the Children's Literature Association, Ann Arbor, Michigan, 17 May 1985.

U 7. "Grand Illusions." Typescript, Sutherland Lecture presented at the University of Chicago, Chicago, Illinois, 4 May 1984.

U 8. "Happily Ever After." Typescript, speech presented at the Carnegie Library, Pittsburgh, Pennsylvania, 7 November 1986.

U 9. "Looking, Listening, and Literature." Typescript, speech presented at the Drexel University Conference, Philadelphia, Pennsylvania, 21 March 1988.

U10. "The Natures and Uses of Fantasy." Typescript, speech presented at the University of Stockholm, Stockholm, Sweden, 24 October 1984.

U11. "Reading as a High-Risk Activity." Typescript, speech presented at the International Reading Association Convention, Philadelphia, Pennsylvania, 15 April 1986.

U12. "Truly Beautiful—or Beautifully True." Children's Literature Conference, Columbus, Ohio, 9 May 1986.

U13. Untitled, unpublished chapter on fantasy. Papers of Dr. Shelton L. Root, Jr., University of Georgia.

B. SECONDARY SOURCES

1. Books and Monographs

B 1. May, Jill P.. *Lloyd Alexander*. Boston: Twayne, forthcoming.

B 2. Rossman, Douglas A. and Charles E. Rossman. *Pages from the Book of III: A Prydain Glossary*. Baltimore: T-K Graphics, 1976.

A brief alphabetical listing of characters, places, and significant objects named in the Prydain Chronicles. Brief explanations are given for each entry as well as a pronunciation guide for Welsh words.

B 3. Tunnell, Michael O. *The Prydain Companion: A Reference Guide to Alexander's Chronicles of Prydain*. New York: Greenwood Press, 1989.

Encyclopedic in format, this work contains entries for characters, places, objects, and themes from the Prydain series. Entries are often lengthy, summarizing information from all the Prydain books and helping readers associate Alexander's life with his books and understand the link between Celtic myth and the modern fantasy story. Includes pronunciation guides for Welsh words. Foreword by Lloyd Alexander.

B 4. Zahorski, Kenneth J. and Robert H. Boyer. *Lloyd Alexander, Evaneline Walton Ensley, Kenneth Morris: A Primary and Secondary Bibliography*. Boston: G.K. Hall, 1981.

This work is a biobibliography of the life and work of Alexander, Ensley, and Morris. A brief biography of Alexander precedes a bibliography of his writings and of the secondary sources that relate to Alexander's work.

2. Dissertations and Studies

D 1. Burns, Linda Lattin. "High Fantasy: A Definition." Diss. University of Missouri—Columbia, 1979.

The purpose of Burns' study is to define High Fantasy. She draws upon Alexander's scholarly writing and heavily upon his Prydain Chronicles as she creates and defends her definition of the genre.

D 2. Halmai, Karolin. "The Chronicles of Prydain: American Mythology in a Celtic Framework." Thesis. Smith College, 1990.

A specialist in Celtic history, Halmai shows the relationships and similarities between modern American attitudes, Alexander's work, and ancient Celtic beliefs.

D 3. Jacobs, James S. "Lloyd Alexander: A Critical Biography." Diss. University of Georgia, 1978.

Jacobs assembled a general biography of Alexander. In addition, he included Alexander's personal philosophy of literature, publishing history, and the critical response to his works.

D 4. McGovern, John Thomas. "Lloyd Alexander—Bard of Prydain: A Study of the Prydain Cycle." Diss. Temple University, 1980.

McGovern's study was designed "to determine if Lloyd Alexander's Chronicles of Prydain, 1) meet the criteria for Heroic Fantasy, 2) use the characters and events of the classic Welsh *Mabinogion* and, 3) adhere to the characteristics found in contemporary High Fantasy."

D 5. Miklovic, Janice. "A Biography-Bibliography of Lloyd Alexander, with an Analysis of Some of His Fantasy Works." Master's Research Paper, Department of Library Science. Kent, Ohio: Kent State University, 1973.

An overview of the life, particularly the writing life, of Lloyd Alexander with commentary on a portion of his writings and their critical reception.

D 6. Sullivan, Charles William III. "The Influence of Celtic Myth and Legend on Modern Imaginative Fiction." Diss. University of Oregon, 1976.

Examination of the general influence of Celtic materials on literature. Alexander's Prydain Chronicles are examined as one of the examples of "the most consistent and conscientious use of the Celtic myths and legends in modern literature."

D 7. Tunnell, Michael O. "An Analytical Companion to Prydain." Diss. Brigham Young University, 1986.

This study is an analytic dictionary containing entries for characters, places, objects, and themes relating to the Prydain Chronicles. Entries summarize information from all Prydain books and tie Alexander's life and Celtic myth to the Prydain story. Pronunciation guides for Welsh words are included.

3. Articles and Book Chapters

C 1.   Adcock, John. "Lloyd Alexander: Wielding the Two-Edged Enchanted Sword." *Starlog*, (December, 1985): 40-41.

Alexander presents his views on his writing, children's literature as a whole, the children who read his books, and the then-forthcoming movie from Disney.

C 2.   Bergman, B.A. "Drexel Hill Author Wins Prize for Children's Book." *Philadelphia Evening Bulletin*, 3 March 1971.

Alexander's activity as an author of children's books is discussed with a focus on his winning the National Book Award.

C 3.   Biscontini, Carol. "Author Enchants the Young with Meaningful Fantasy." *Philadelphia Inquirer*, 3 June 1984.

This look at Alexander's writing life centers on Prydain and the local school children as they respond to the man and his works.

C 4.   Bisenieks, Dainis. "Tales from the 'Perilous Realm': Good News for the Modern Child." *Christian Century*, 91, 5 June, 1974, pp. 617-620.

Bisenieks explores some strengths of three writers of fantasy: Tolkien, Alexander and LeGuin. He uses examples from Prydain which he found moving, discusses the growth of the main character, and shows how great literature teaches in a way different from the instruction in lesser works.

C 5.   Braude, Anne. "Interview: Lloyd Alexander." Niekas: *The Awfset Fanzine*, 23 (August 1980): 19-24.

The focus of this interview is upon Alexander's attitude toward fantasy in general and Prydain in particular.

C 6.   Carr, Marion. "Classic Hero in a New Mythology." *Horn Book*, 47 (October 1971): 508-513.

Taran, Alexander's high fantasy hero, is examined in light of Jan de Vries' ten motifs that characterize a traditional and classic hero. Taran is found to operate within eight of the ten motifs.

C 7.   Clark, Hattie. "His Children's Books Explore Clash Between Good and Evil." *Christian Science Monitor*, 8 July 1985, pp. 25-26.

Background and awards of Alexander are treated, with a focus on daily activities of the author.

C 8. Clegg, Paula K. "A Gift from Lloyd Alexander." *Cricket*, 17 (November 1989): 47-49.

The author tells of her childhood passion for the books of Lloyd Alexander, especially the Prydain Chronicles, and of her visit to Alexander's home when she was twelve. It was a dream come true. "He gave me the insight that an author is made of flesh and blood instead of fantasy."

C 9. Colbath, Mary Lou. "Worlds as They Should Be: Middle-earth, Narnia and Prydain." *Elementary English*, (December 1971): 937-945.

The author calls Tolkien's Lord of the Rings, Lewis' Chronicles of Narnia, and Alexander's Chronicles of Prydain "three great works" within an unique area of fantasy writing characterized by secondary worlds, mythological heritage, and special stimulants to the imagination (adventure, enchantments, heroism).

C10. Commire, Anne, ed. "Lloyd Alexander." *Something About the Author*, Vol. 3. Detroit: Gale, 1972, pp. 7-9.

Commire lists information about Alexander in encyclopedic format: personal data, publication history, excerpts from speeches and articles, critical commentary on works.

C11. Cramer, Barbara B. "Bequest of Wings: Three Readers and Special Books." *Language Arts*, 61 (March 1984): 253-260.

Within this article, Cramer interviews Mike, a seventh grade boy, about his reading of *The High King* in an attempt to illustrate the importance of reader response to literature.

C12. Durell, Ann. "Lloyd Alexander: Newbery Winner." *School Library Journal*, 15 (15 May 1969): 2066-2068.

In this autobiographical recounting of the relationship between Editor Durell and Author Alexander, the emphasis is the development of Prydain and its recent completion and honors.

C13. Durell, Ann. "Who's Lloyd Alexander?" *Horn Book*, 47 (August 1969): 382-384.

Durell recalls the initial impressions some people have had about Alexander, including her own. Her summary: Everyone was correct, plus "Lloyd is all the characters in his books, sometimes in turn, sometimes all at once."

C14. Eby, Eleanor. "Alexander's Wizardry Is Honored Once More." *Philadelphia Inquirer*, 27 July 1975.

Eby, Children's Book Reviewer for the Inquirer, conducts a short basic interview.

C15. Evans, W.E. Emrys. "The Welsh Mabinogion: Tellings and Retellings." *Children's Literature in Education*, 9, No. 1 (Spring 1978): 17-33.

Evans examines Alexander's Chronicles of Prydain, Garner's *The Owl Service*, and Walton's *Books of the Welsh Mabinogion*, plus some versions of the Welsh tales taken from the Four Branches of the *Mabinogion*. He evaluates Prydain's connection to the Mabinogion ("very free") as well as the books themselves. He finds it a good story, though would not have awarded it the Newbery Medal.

C16. Fine, Mary Jane. "Cameras, Children and Curiosity." *Philadelphia Inquirer*, 12 June 1984.

A fourth grade class from Samuel Gompers Elementary in Philadelphia videotaped an interview with Alexander for a segment of *Children's Magazine*.

C17. Glass, Rona. "A Wrinkle in Time and The High King: Two Couples, Two Perspectives." *Children's Literature Association Quarterly*, 6 (Fall 1981): 15-18.

In both of these Newbery-winning novels is a main character "involved throughout the story with a close, beloved friend of the opposite sex"—Meg Murry and Calvin O'Keefe, Taran and Eilonwy. Glass examines the influence of these relationships on the protagonists' decisions to undertake their quests..

C18. Gordon, Suzanne. "Children's Fantasies Turn to Gold for Drexel Hill's Lloyd Alexander." *Philadelphia Bulletin*, 20 March 1978.

Gordon presents a general interview dealing with Alexander's writing history and awards.

C19. "The Gothic Style of Disney." *Life*, 1 (November 1978): 99.

This brief update on the forthcoming animated epic, *The Black Cauldron*, promises it will be a "Disney's answer to *The Lord of the Rings*."

C20. Greenlaw, Jean. "Profile: Lloyd Alexander." *Language Arts*, 61 (April 1984): 406-413.

Greenlaw's interview was conducted with questions from fifth grade students at Brandenburg Elementary School, Irving, Texas.

C21. Hopkins, Lee Bennett. "Lloyd Alexander." In *More Books by More People*. New York: Citation Press, 1974, pp. 10-18.

Hopkins introduces Lloyd Alexander in this short biographical piece which begins with an introduction to Alexander's Prydain. Often quoting Alexander, Hopkins reviews highlights of the author's life story, especially as it relates to his writing.

C22. Jacobs, James S. "A Personal Look at Lloyd Alexander." *The Advocate*, 4 (Fall 1984): 8-18.

Drawing from his biographical research about Lloyd Alexander, Jacobs shows the connections between Alexander's life and his writing. Many interesting details concerning Alexander's background and work habits are shared.

C23. Kiefer, Barbara Z. "Wales as a Setting for Children's Fantasy." *Children's Literature in Education*, 13, No. 2 (Summer 1982): 95-102.

The author links the geography of Wales to children's fantasy set in Wales. She zeroes in on Alexander's *The High King*, Garner's *The Owl Service*, and Cooper's *The Grey King*. She identifies Prydainian geography, such as the Isle of Mona (island of Anglesey) and the "Eagle's Nest" in the Snowdonia Mountains, but she feels the geographical link is weak in the Prydain books.

C24. Kuznets, Lois R. "'High Fantasy' in America: A Study of Lloyd Alexander, Ursula LeGuin and Susan Cooper." *The Lion and the Unicorn*, 9 (1985): 19-35.

After a brief look at the history of fantasy writing in America, Kuznets examines and compares the works of Alexander, LeGuin, and Cooper to see how the "Arthurian myth of male development" is used (and misused) in each author's books.

C25. Lane, Elizabeth. "Lloyd Alexander's Chronicles of Prydain and the Welsh Tradition." *Orcrist*, 7 (1973): 25-29.

Lane traces the roots of Celtic myth that anchor the Prydain Chronicles. She examines characters and events drawn from the *Mabinogion*, a collection of ancient Welsh tales, and reworked by Alexander in his high fantasy series.

C26. Lewis, Donna Williams. "Fantasy Author Alexander Emerges in Person for Pupils." *Intown Extra*, Atlanta, Georgia, 23 May 1985.

Lewis reports Lloyd Alexander's visit to Cook and Westminster Elementary Schools in Atlanta, Georgia. Samples of answers to questions posed by the students are included, plus a brief history of Alexander's publishing record.

C27. "Lloyd Alexander in Lexington, Massachusetts." *Horn Book*, 47 (February 1971): 102-103.

This brief article reports Lloyd Alexander's visit to the Maria Hastings Elementary School in Lexington, Massachusetts, and the school's preparations for receiving their guest. Samples of children's thank you letters are included.

C28. Maggitti, Phil. "The Man Who (Sometimes) Wishes to be a Cat." *Cats Magazine*, 43 (April 1986): 18-21.

The Alexander household became a haven for cats as soon as the couple bought a house, and cats also have been a part of Lloyd's writing. Maggitti discusses the real and fictional cats in Lloyd's life.

C29. Malone, Ruth. "Lloyd Alexander At Home: Things Are Under Control—Except for William." Drexel Hill Press, 23 August 1989.

This human interest article looks at a local author, his household, cats, and writing career.

C30. "A Man Who's Written His Own Ticket." *Philadelphia Inquirer*, 17 August 1989, p. 24 DC.

This is an update of various articles about Lloyd Alexander printed in Philadelphia newspapers over the years. It takes a look at Alexander's life and his successful writing career.

C31. McMillen, Dorothy. "Love of Violin Inspired Award-Winning Book." *Philadelphia Bulletin*, 3 June 1971.

Standard interview with an emphasis on *The Marvelous Misadventures of Sebastian* and its winning the National Book Award.

C32. "Meet Your Author." *Cricket*, 1 (September 1973): 76.

Alexander's answers to a list of somewhat personal questions—What is your favorite food?—provides readers with a glimpse into the life of the author.

C33. Murphy, Bill. "Author Alexander Takes Another Flight Into Fantasy." News of Delaware County, 2 August 1989.

Murphy presents a brief overview of Alexander's writing career.

C34. "NBA Winner Stresses Seriousness of Fantasy." *Library Journal*, 96 (17 February 1969): 1412-1413.

In these excerpts of Alexander's acceptance speech for the National Book Award, he pointed out how fantasy can address directly the realistic issues of the contemporary world; that fantasy explores the reality of life. The article is followed by the challenge of George Woods that the NBA nominees were "mostly pottage."

C35. "The Newbery-Caldecott Secret—Not a Secret Anymore." *Publishers'*
      Weekly, 195 (17 February 1969): 129-130.

      The year Alexander received the Newbery Medal, the procedure for
      naming the winner was changed from waiting two months to an
      immediate announcement. Brief comment on *The High King* and a
      brief writing history of Alexander accompanied that information.

C36. Nikolajeva, Maria. "Amerikanskii Bard Lloyd Alexander." *Detskaya*
      Literatura (Moscow), May, 1988, pp. 40-42. (In Russian.)

      Alexander draws upon ancient European mythology, folk materials,
      and historical elements to create a new American mythology.

C37. Painter, Helen W. "Lloyd Alexander: The Man and His Books for
      Children."   In *Reaching Children and Young People through*
      Literature. Ed. Helen W. Painter. Newark, Delaware: International
      Reading Association, 1971, pp. 30-36.

      Painter has compiled a biographical account of Alexander, focusing
      primarily on his writing history.

C38. Patterson, Nancy-Lou. "Homo Monstrosus: Gurgi and Other Shadow
      Figures in Fantastic Literature." *Mythlore*, 3, no. 11: 24.

      After listing minor criticisms of the Prydain Chronicles, the author
      lauds Alexander's work and specifically what he has done with the
      archetypal monster figure of Gurgi. She examines the "shadow
      figures" of fantasy literature and compares them to Gurgi, explaining
      what such characters might represent.

C39. Reasoner, Charles F. "A Teacher's Guide to the Paperback Editions of
      the Prydain Chronicles by Lloyd Alexander." New York: Dell, 1982.

      Produced by the publisher and available to teachers, this pamphlet
      provides some information about Alexander, academic views Prydain,
      and some exercises and activities for classroom use.

C40. Schickel, Richard. "PG Thrills in the Land of Legend." *Time*, (29 July
      1985): 68.

      Schickel sums up the new Disney movie, finding it worthwhile.

C41. "SLJ Meets Lloyd Alexander." *School Library Journal*, 96 (15 April
      1971): 1421-1423.

      Interview written in question-and-answer form centering upon
      Alexander's literary views, work habits, interest in music, anti-war
      views, and ability to comment on the real world in fantasy writing.

C42.   Stott, Jon C.   "Alexander's Chronicles of Prydain: The Nature of Beginnings."   In *Touchstones: Reflections of the Best in Children's Literature, Volume 1.*   Ed. Perry Nodelman.   Purdue University, West Lafayette, Indiana: Children's Literature Association, 1985, pp. 21-29.

After summarizing the plot and introducing the characters of the Prydain Chronicles, Stott examines Prydain as an example of the *Bildungsroman* to see what Alexander has done to make his version of an old theme of such high quality.

C43.   Stuart, Dee.   "An Exclusive Interview with Lloyd Alexander."   *Writer's Digest*, 53 (April 1973): 33-35+.

"My aim in writing for children is consciousness raising . . . to foster compassion . . . to speak to the adult in the child.   Books are our approach to life through art."   General interview with Alexander dealing with work habits, response to awards, definition of fantasy and views of literature.

C44.   Sutherland, Zena.   "Captive Author, Captivated Audience."   *Saturday Review*, 55 (22 April 1972): 78.

The author reports on a visit by Alexander to students at University of Chicago's Laboratory School.   Alexander responded to many questions and concluded: "You know, they asked most of the same questions my students ask—and they're in graduate school!"

C45.   Toijer-Nilsson, Ying.   "Att förbrylla, tjusa, uppröra."   In *Fantasins Underland*.   Klippan, Sweden: Efs, 1981, pp. 110-126.   (In Swedish.)

This is a survey and interpretation of major works including the Prydain Chronicles and *The Marvelous Misadventure of Sebastian* and *The First Two Lives of Lukas-Kasha*.   The author relates the books to events in the United States and elsewhere in the world.

C46.   Treadway, Dean.   "Anything But A Sprawling Disney Epic."   *Signal* (6 August 1985): 8.

For all the effort, time, and expense put into the production of Disney's *The Black Cauldron*, the result left much to be desired "refusing to give Lloyd Alexander's books the fully grand and lengthy treatment they deserved."   Those who saw the movie "missed something that the movie didn't provide in the first place: grounds for caring about its heroes."

C47.	Tunnell, Michael O. "An Interview with Lloyd Alexander." *The New Advocate*, 2 (Spring 1989): 83-95.

Lloyd Alexander responds to questions concerning his writing and his other interests.

C48.	Tunnell, Michael O. "Profile: Eilonwy of the Red-gold Hair." *Language Arts*, 66 (September 1989): 558-563.

Eilonwy from the Prydain Chronicles is a character who helped introduce a new breed of less stereotypical females to children's literature. Her qualities of wisdom, courage, straightforwardness, independence of spirit, leadership and resourcefulness, and being a good person (and still being undeniably female) are examined.

C49.	Tunnell, Michael O. and James S. Jacobs. "Alexander's Chronicles of Prydain: Twenty Years Later." *School Library Journal*, 34 (April 1988): 27-31.

The authors celebrate the twentieth anniversary of the Prydain Chronicles by examining its popularity and by recounting the events spanning several years which led to the publication of the fantasy series. Elements that make the series outstanding are also examined.

C50.	Tunnell, Michael O. and James S. Jacobs. "Fantasy at Its Best: Alexander's Chronicles of Prydain." *Children's Literature in Education*, in press.

Reasons for the enduring popularity of Alexander's Prydain Chronicles are discussed. Four basic characteristics of Prydain that seem to affect its longevity are examined: credibility, tension, humor, and hope.

C51.	West, Richard C. "The Tolkinians." *Orcrist*, 2 (1967/68): 4-15.

West dubs Alan Garner, Carol Kendall, and Lloyd Alexander as "The Tolkinians," and describes Prydain as a "mixture of Tolkien and T. H. White." He then looks at Prydain's connections with Welsh mythology.

C52.	Whetton, Betty B. "Who Will Read Prydain?" *Arizona English Bulletin*, 14 (Spring 1972): 51-53.

An eighth grade teacher found that her students would read Prydain, but did not want to talk about the books. She surmised they did not want to be labeled as fairy tale readers and concludes that Prydain is not just for younger readers.

C53. Wintle, Justin and Emma Fisher. "Lloyd Alexander." *The Pied Pipers.*
New York: Paddington Press, 1974, pp. 208-220.

Included as one of the most influential contemporary writers for
children, Alexander responds to questions about his art and life.

4. Book Reviews

a. Adult audience

Fifty Years in the Doghouse

R 1. Allen, W. H. "Two-footed Friend." *Punch*, 246, 19 May 1965, p. 752.
(Review of *Send for Ryan!*)

"Lloyd Alexander tells dozens of good stories in the perfect throwaway
manner."

R 2. Binns, Frederic W. "Review." *Library Journal*, 89 (15 February 1964):
856.

Favorable review.

R 3. Kenney, Harry C. "Act of Kindness." *Christian Science Monitor*, 6
February 1964, p. 9.

"[A] warmhearted, amusing account of Bill Ryan's incredible true
adventures."

Janine is French

R 4. Brace, Joan. "Homesick But Gay Parisian." *Chicago Sunday Tribune*,
15 March 1969, p. 4.

"[T]he whole texture of the book is charged with a convincing
tenderness rarely found in such once-over-lightly treatments . . . ."

R 5. Feld, Rose. "Parisienne in Pennsylvania." *New York Herald Tribune
Book Review*, 22 March 1959, p. 6.

"[A] portrait that has an engaging, gamine quality."

R 6. Gilbert, Morris. "The Accent is Gallic." *New York Times Book Review*, 22 March 1959, p. 33.

      Mixed review. "Hardly a living wife can boast of being as assiduously analyzed, documented and affectionately chronicled in print. . . . It is unfortunate that . . . so many of the episodes develop as farce."

R 7. Grandchamp, Aline de. "His Wife is from France." *Christian Science Monitor*, 4 May 1959, p. 14.

      Favorable review.

R 8. Hart, Lyn. "Review." *Library Journal*, 84 (1 April 1959): 1123.

      "[Janine] is so finely caught in the pages of the book by her husband."

R 9. "Review." *Kirkus*, 27 (15 February 1959): 159.

      Favorable review.

R10. Lux, Louise. "Meet the Alexanders—and Their Cats." *Philadelphia Sunday Bulletin*, 22 March 1959.

      Favorable review.

R11. "Review." *New Yorker*, 35 (28 March 1959): 156.

      Favorable review.

My Five Tigers

R12. Beecroft, John. "How to Get on with a Cat." *New York Herald Tribune Book Review*, 25 March 1956, p. 3.

      Favorable review.

R13. "Review." *Booklist*, 52 (1 March 1956): 266.

      Favorable review.

R14. Freedley, George. "Review." *Library Journal*, 80 (1 December 1955): 2764.

      Favorable review.

R15. "Review." *Kirkus*, 23 (1 December 1955): 884.

      Favorable review.

R16. Lockridge, Richard. "Kittens and Cats." *New York Times Book Review*, 12 February 1956, p. 12.

"It is a gay book—funny often, as gracefully written as all books about cats should be."

R17. McDowell, Laura E., and Melvin G. Reed. "Review." *Bookmark*, 15 (February 1956): 104.

Favorable review.

R18. "Review." *New Yorker*, 31 (11 February 1956): 120.

"A pleasant, whimsical, careful trifle . . ."

R19. T., N.E. "Concourse of Cats." *Christian Science Monitor*, 29 March 1956, p. 7.

"Although Mr. Alexander has remarked that the reasons for a cat's appeal to us 'can never be expressed too clearly,' has has managed to come very close to capturing in words that elusive fascination."

My Love Affair with Music

R20. B., D.B. "Review." *Sunday Republican.* (Springfield, Massachusetts), 3 July 1960, p. 5D.

Favorable review.

R21. "Review." *Booklist*, 56 (15 May 1960): 563.

"An enjoyable autobiographical excursion . . .that reveals a sense of humor and a fascination for music . . . ."

R22. Dolson, Hildegarde. "Music Was His Mistress." *New York Times Book Review*, 29 May 1960, p. 9.

"[S]uch an enchanting, witty little book . . . [written] in words that seem to grow as naturally and gracefully as leaves on a tree . . . ."

R23. "Review." *Horn Book*, 27 (August 1960): 317.

Favorable review.

R24. Johnson, Gerald. "What's This? Music for the Fun of It?" *New York Herald Tribune Book Review*, 22 May 1960, p. 5.

"[I]t is fun to follow his erratic career . . . for if his comments are never reverential they are always shrewd and embody a great deal of too-much-neglected truth."

R25. "Review." *Kirkus*, 28 (1 March 1960): 228.

Mixed review. "A loose collection of reminiscences, which, though they alternate pleasingly between sadness and gaiety, lack the substance one hopes to find in a full length book."

R26. Miller, Catharine K. "Review." *Library Journal*, 85 (15 March 1960): 1120.

Favorable review.

R27. "Review." *Philadelphia Bulletin*, 14 July 1960.

Favorable review.

b. Young audience

The Beggar Queen

R28. Barham, Carole A. "Review." *Voice of Youth Advocates*, 9 (June 1986): 105.

Favorable review.

R29. "Review." *The Best in Children's Books: The University of Chicago Guide to Children's Literature, 1979-1984*. Ed. Zena Sutherland. Chicago: The University of Chicago Press, 1986, p. 10.

Starred review. ". . . [a] fine piece of craftsmanship . . . ."

R30. "Review." *Booklist*, 80 (15 April 1984): 1186.

Starred review. "The chronicle begun in *Westmark* and carried through *The Kestrel* is brought to a brilliant climax in a novel that skillfully completes this landmark trilogy . . . . [T]he trilogy has remarkable depth and symmetry . . . ."

R31. "Review." *Bulletin of the Center for Children's Books*, 37 (May 1984): 159.

Starred review. ". . . [a] fine piece of craftsmanship . . . a story that has pace, polished style, and suspense."

R32. Burns, Mary M. "Review." *Horn Book*, 60 (August 1984): 472.

"[R]esolves the fates of the characters through a surprising, carefully wrought climax. Although references to earlier events are smoothly integrated into the text, they cannot fully convey the skill of the author's complicated, fully realized characterizations."

R33. Donovan, Diane C. "Review." *Best Sellers*, 44 (September 1984): 228.

Favorable review.

R34. "Good Books to Give to Kids." *Changing Times*, 38 (December 1984): 69.

Favorable review.

R35. "Review." *Children's Book Review Service*, 12 (June 1984): 116.

Favorable review.

R36. Hoffman, Elizabeth P. "Children's Literature in 1984." *Catholic Library World*, 56 (October 1984): 126.

Favorable review.

R37. "Review." *Horn Book*, 62 (July 1986): 473.

Favorable review.

R38. Jacobs, James S. "Review." *BYU Children's Book Review*, 4 (May/June 1984): 11.

Favorable review.

R39. Jones, Trev. "Review." *School Library Journal*, 30 (March 1984): 168.

"[M]agnificent conclusion to [Westmark] trilogy. . . . The rich characterization . . . is deftly interwoven in this exciting adventure that is told with tongue-in-cheek humor and eloquent language."

R40. "Review." *Journal of Reading*, 28 (February 1985): 470.

Favorable review.

R41. "Review." Kliatt Young Adult Paperback Book Guide, 20 (Winter 1986): 4.

Favorable review.

R42. Kennemer, Phyllis. "Review." *Language Arts*, 62 (February 1985): 196.

Critics choice. "Appreciation of these books escalates as they are reread."

R43. "Review." *Learning*, 13 (November 1984): 71.

Favorable review.

R44. Moore, Teresa. "Area Booksellers Name Their Favorite Titles." *Book World* (*Washington Post*), 18 (8 May 1988): 16-17.

Favorable review.

R45. "Review." *New Directions for Women*, 14 (July 1985): 16.

Favorable review.

R46. Nix, Kemie. "Review." *The Advocate*, 5 (Winter/Spring 1986): 217.

Favorable review.

R47. Nix, Kemie. "Review." *Atlanta Journal-Constitution*, 6 May 1984, p. 10H.

Favorable review.

R48. Nix, Kemie. "Review." *Atlanta Journal-Constitution*, 23 March 1986, pp. 8J.

Favorable review.

R49. Nix, Kemie. "Review." *Parents' Choice* (Fall/Winter 1985), p. 16.

Favorable review.

R50. Nix, Kemie. "Review." *Parents' Choice* (Holidays 1985), p. 14.

Favorable review.

R51. "Review." *Publishers' Weekly*, 225 (11 May 1984): 273.

Favorable review.

R52. "Review." *Reading Teacher*, 38 (October 1984): 92.

Favorable review.

R53. Thompson, Raymond. "Review." *Fantasy Review*, 7 (November 1984): 44.

"Fine control of style, exciting pace, and a varied cast of characters complement a thoughtful theme. Highly recommended to all younger readers and libraries that serve them."

R54. Yates, Diane. "Review." *Voice of Youth Advocates*, 7 (October 1984): 204.

"Alexander is a master at building suspense . . . [and] provides food for the thoughtful reader. . . . Sure to be on the Best Books List; a candidate for the Newbery Award."

The Black Cauldron

R55. "Review." *Booklist*, 62 (1 September 1965): 52.

"A wise and wonderful tale written in epic fashion."

R56. "Review." *Books and Bookmen*, 18 (May 1973): 125.

Favorable review (with *The Book of Three*).

R57. "Review." *Bookweek* (9 May 1965): 12, 14.

"There is a sense of genuine enthusiasm for old Welsh Faerie in his books, an ability to fashion an interesting plot with magical elements and a fine light style but so far he seems to us to have not quite brought it off."

R58. "Review." *Fantasy Review*, 8 (October 1985): 27.

"[T]his reprint is intended as a lure. The cover illustration would suggest to the reader that here is the text of the Disney film. . . . The young reader may at first be disappointed to find that the book bears very little resemblance to the film, but Alexander's story is so good that the effort may succeed beyond expectations. If the garish cover brings one reader to the enjoyment of the entire Prydain series, one can but praise the effort."

R59. Fritz, Jean. "For Young Readers." *New York Times Book Review*, 19 June 1966, p. 36.

Favorable review (with *The Book of Three* and *The Castle of Llyr*).

R60. Izard, Anne. "New Books for Children." *Grade Teacher*, 83 (May/June 1966): 33.

Favorable review.

R61. "Review." *Kirkus*, 33 (1 April 1965): 377.

Starred review. " . . . the kind of once-in-a-lifetime reading that will assure Prydain a permanent place in geographies of fictional territories."

R62. Leland, Dorothy E. "Review." *Parents*, 41 (August 1966): 70.

Favorable review.

R63. "Review." *London Times Literary Supplement*, 25 May 1967, p. 450.

Mixed review. ". . . story . . . is exciting and well-constructed . . . . Unfortunately the author tries too hard to be funny as well as dramatic, and the result is a forced flippancy . . . ."

R64. "Review." *London Times Literary Supplement*, 6 April 1973, p. 379.

Favorable review (with *The Book of Three*).

R65. Seacord, Laura F. "Review." *Library Journal*, 90 (15 April 1965): 2017.

"A brisk adventure story with a satisfying blend of fantasy and humor."

R66. Sutherland, Zena. "Review." *Bulletin of the Center for Children's Books*, 19 (January 1966): 77.

"[A] satisfying wholeness of artistic conception, a graceful style, humor in dialogue and in characterization, and a robust sense of adventure."

R67. V., R.H. "Review." *Horn Book*, 41 (June 1965): 274.

"An exalting experience for the fortunate children whose imaginations are ready for great fantasy."

R68. Yates, Jessica. "Review." *Times Educational Supplement*, 6 June 1986, p. 50.

Favorable review (with *The Book of Three*).

The Book of Three

R69. "Review." *Booklist*, 61 (1 December 1964): 344, 346.

"Filled with exciting and valorous action, humor and truth . . . ."

R70. "Review." *Books and Bookmen,* 18 (May 1973): 125.

Favorable review (with *The Black Cauldron*).

R71. "Review." *Bookweek,* (29 November 1964) : 28

"[T]hese are carefully imagined tales written with considerable skill."

R72. "Review." *Book World,* 11 (10 May 1981): 14.

Favorable review.

R73. Dodson, Marguerite A. "Review." *Library Journal,* 79 (15 September 1964): 3465.

Favorable review.

R74. "Review." *Emergency Librarian,* 11 (January 1984): 20.

Favorable review.

R75. Fritz, Jean. "Review." *New York Times Book Review,* 71, 19 June 1966, p. 36.

Favorable review (with *The Black Cauldron* and *The High King*).

R76. Lewis, Naomi. "Review." *Observer* (London), 27 November 1966, p. 28.

Favorable review.

R77. Monico, David. "No Jet-Set Robots in This Fairy Tale." *Catholic Herald* (London), 30 September 1966.

"[Alexander] is to be congratulated on all counts."

R78. "Review." *New Catholic World,* 216, March 1973, p. 92.

Favorable review.

R79. "Review." *New York Review of Books.* 3 December 1964, p. 16.

"[T]he tone of the narrative is brisk and down-to-earth . . . ."

R80. "Review." *Observer* (London), 5 January 1986, p. 43.

Favorable review.

R81. Sutherland, Zena. "Review." *Bulletin of the Center for Children's Books*, 18 (July/August 1965): 157.

"A long, complicated, imaginative, and very funny adventure tale. . . ."

R82. "Review." *London Times Literary Supplement*, 24 November 1966, p. 1089.

Favorable review.

R83. "Review." *London Times Literary Supplement*, 6 April 1973, p. 379.

"[A] superb invention . . . a rich alliance of humour, terror, wit, ideas . . . ."

R84. "Review." *Times Educational Supplement*, 29 July 1988, p. 21.

"I don't know how I missed this increasingly impressive saga of the making of a king before, but I recommend it now to all with an insatiable Tolkien-hunger; it's funny, too."

R85. V., R.H. "Folktales and Fanciful Stories." *Horn Book*, 40 (October 1964): 496.

"[T]he book will wear well, and children will be eager for other stories in which Taran may yet learn the meaning of heroism."

R86. Yates, Jessica. "Review." *Times Educational Supplement*, 6 June 1986, p. 50.

"Apart from Taran, who grows from boy to man, the supporting characters have predictable reactions, yet there is some variety in the humour, and the adventures in each volume, shaped around a Quest."

Border Hawk: August Bondi

R87. Brody, Julia Jussim. "Review." *Library Journal*, 83 (15 May 1958): 1599.

Favorable review.

R88. "Review." *Commonweal*, 68 (23 May 1958): 215.

"[V]ery well done and inspiring . . . ."

R89. K., M.B. "Jews in Early America." *Chicago Sunday Tribune*, 11 May 1958, p. 9.

Favorable review.

R90. Ribalow, Harold U. "Fighters for Freedom." *New York Times Book Review*, 23 March 1958, p. 36.

"[T]he author manages to inject—painlessly and usefully—thoughts about liberty, Americanism and the values of Judaism."

R91. "Review." *San Francisco Chronicle*, 11 May 1958, p. 24.

Favorable review.

The Castle of Llyr

R92. "Review." *The Best in Children's Books: The University of Chicago Guide to Children's Literature, 1966-1972.* Ed. Zena Sutherland. Chicago: University of Chicago Press, 1973, p. 6.

"A third delightful book about the land of Prydain . . . . The author has conceived his legendary land in the whole: the characters fit the plot, the plot fits the style of writing, and the style of writing fits the genre."

R93. "Review." *Booklist*, 62 (1 July 1966): 1042.

Favorable review.

R94. Fritz, Jean. "Review." *New York Times Book Review*, 19 June 1966, p. 36.

Favorable review (with *The Book of Three* and *The Black Cauldron*).

R95. Kilpatrick, Elizabeth Gross. "Review." *Childhood Educator*, 63 (February 1967): 354.

Favorable review.

R96. King, Martha Bennett. "Review." *Books Today* (Chicago Tribune), 7 August 1966, p. 11.

"Flashes of humor, glisten of tears, whisper of wisdom adorn the taut prose which drives a tense tale to a happy ending."

R97. "Review." *Kirkus*, 34 (15 March 1966): 301.

"Character and dialogue is handled humorously and dexterously, which sets this classic-in-the-making apart from other folklore-based fantasies."

R98. Libby, Margaret Sherwood. "Types of Fantasy." *Bookweek* (August 21, 1966): 11.

Mixed review. " . . . elaborately mythical adventures of odd and comical, if somewhat stilted, characters . . . ."

R99. "Review." *London Times Literary Supplement*, 3 October 1968, p. 1113.

"The climax is fierce and perilous indeed but touched with great humanity. . . ."

R100. Ostermann, Robert. "Mr. Alexander Returns to Prydain—Where Evil is 'Never Distant!'" *National Observer*, 19 December 1966, p. 19.

"[T]esting of his characters . . . [gives] his fantasies a dimension lacking in the usual fairy-tale adventure."

R101. "Review." *Publishers' Weekly*, 189 (23 May 1966): 83.

Favorable review.

R102. Rausen, Ruth. "Review." *Library Journal*, 91 (15 April 1966): 2205.

Favorable review.

R103. Russ, Lavinia. "Review." *Publishers' Weekly*, 189 (23 May 1966): 83.

Favorable review.

R104. Shaw, Spencer G. "Review." *Top of the News*, 23 (January 1967): 195.

Favorable review.

R105. Sutherland, Zena. "Review." *Bulletin of the Center for Children's Books*, 20 (February 1967): 85.

"[T]he characters fit the plot, the plot fits the style of writing, and the style of writing fits the genre."

R106. V., R.H. "Review." *Horn Book*, 42 (June 1966): 304-305.

Favorable review.

The Cat Who Wished to be a Man

R107. Andrejevic, Helen. "Books for Boys and Girls." *Parents*, 48, November 1973, p. 89.

"Lloyd Alexander has combined adventure, humor, and an unblinking eye for human foibles to produce a lighthearted allegory of distinction."

R108. "Review." *The Best in Children's Books: The University of Chicago Guide to Children's Literature, 1973-1978.* Ed. Zena Sutherland. Chicago: The University of Chicago Press, 1980, p. 8.

"[T]he style, the humor, the play on words, the rumbustious characters, and the pace of the action are delightful."

R109. "Review." *Booklist,* 70 (1 October 1973): 168.

"[E]xuberant, tongue-in-cheek commentary on human foibles,"

R110. "Review." *Booklist,* 70 (15 March, 1974): 826.

Favorable review.

R111. Goodwin, June. "Review." *Christian Science Monitor,* 7 November 1973, p. B5.

"It is slightly pretentious—trying too hard to be a fantasy—and fails to hold the reader's interest."

R112. Heins, Ethel L. "Review." *Horn Book,* 49 (October 1973): 463-464.

"A comic and ebullient fantasy just right for reading aloud."

R113. Kellman, Amy. "Review." *Top of the News,* 30 (January 1974): 205.

Favorable review.

R114. "Review." *Kirkus,* 41 (15 June 1973): 639.

Favorable review.

R115. Long, Sidney. "Review." *New York Times Book Review,* 30 September 1973, p. 10.

"[I]t is a concoction rather than a creation."

R116. "Review." *New Yorker,* 49 (3 December 1973): 205.

Mixed review.

R117. Nix, Kemie. "Review." *Parents' Choice* (Fall/Winter 1980), p. 10.

Favorable review.

R118. "Review." *Publishers' Weekly,* 204 (16 July 1973): 111.

Favorable review.

R119. "Review." *Saturday Review World*, 1 (4 December 1973): 28.

Favorable review.

R120. Silver, Linda R. "Review." *Library Journal*, 98 (15 September 1973): 2647.

"Infused with humor, high spirits and compassion . . . recognizes mankind's many frailties without despairing and offers hope that love and justice sometimes prevail."

R121. Sutherland, Zena. "Review." *Bulletin of the Center for Children's Books*, 27 (October 1973): 21.

"The plot is not highly original in basic concept . . . but the style, the humor, the play on words, the rumbustious characters, and the pace of the action are delightful."

R122. "Review." *Teacher*, 91 (March 1974): 109.

Favorable review.

Coll and His White Pig

R123. "Review." *Booklist*, 62 (15 December 1965): 407.

Favorable review.

R124. D., P.M. "Review." *Christian Science Monitor*, 31 March 1966, p. 15.

Favorable review.

R125. "Review." *Grade Teacher* (January 1966): 22.

Favorable review.

R126. "Review." *Grade Teacher* (October 1971): 96.

Favorable review.

R127. "Review." *Kirkus*, 33 (1 November 1965): 1115.

Favorable review.

R128. Libby, Margaret Sherwood. "Helping Hands, and Feet." *Bookweek* (30 January 1966): 16.

Favorable review.

R129. Mosel, Arlene. "Review." *Library Journal*, 90 (15 December 1965): 5506.

"For the imaginative reader, perhaps the somewhat rare one, sensitive to beauty."

R130. "Review." *New Yorker*, (4 December 1971): 180.

Favorable review.

R131. O'Doherty, Barbara Novak. "Review." *New York Times Book Review*, part 2, 7 November 1965, p. 62.

Favorable review.

R132. Sutherland, Zena. "Review." *Bulletin of the Center for Children's Books*, 19 (January 1966): 77.

"The writing style is good, although the author's elegance and subtlety are not as appropriate for younger children as they are for the upper-grades readers."

R133. V., R.H. "Review." *Horn Book*, 41 (December 1965): 619.

Favorable review.

The Drackenberg Adventure

R134. Andronik, Catherine. "Review." *Book Report*, 7 (November 1988): 33.

"This latest adventure will appeal to old fans [of Vesper Holly] and win new ones."

R135. C., I. "Review." *Booklist*, 84 (1 May 1988): 1514.

Starred review. "As usual, Alexander is to be commended for his elegant writing, astute characterizations, and his presentation of an intelligent heroine."

R136. Dow, Sally R. "Review." *School Library Journal*, 34 (June 1988): 99.

Favorable review.

R137. Greenlaw, Jean. "Review." *The New Advocate*, 1 (Spring 1988): 278.

Favorable review.

R138. Heins, Ethel L. "Review." *Horn Book*, 64 (July 1988): 499.

"With its wonderfully exaggerated characters, tantalizing chapter endings, literate style, and witty repartee, the book—probably the best of the trilogy—must have been almost as much fun to write as it is the read."

R139. Jacobs, James S. "Review." *BYU Children's Book Review*, 8 (May/June 1988): 6.

Favorable review.

R140. "Review." *Kirkus*, 56 (1 April 1988): 533.

Favorable review.

R141. "Review." *Publishers' Weekly*, 233 (29 April 1988): 78.

"Deft storytelling combines with thorough research to create a seamless, fantastic vision of 19th century life."

R142. S., L. "Review." *Reading Teacher*, 43 (November 1989): 155.

Favorable review.

R143. Sebesta, Sam L., Diane Monson and Peggy Compston. "Review." *Reading Teacher*, 42 (November 1988): 164.

Favorable review.

R144. Sutherland, Zena. "Review." *Bulletin of the Center for Children's Books*, 41 (June 1988): 197.

"Adventures galore, humor as usual, colorful (if not wholly convincing) characters, and the appeal of a series book are combined in a story written with the typical Alexandrian gusto and aplomb."

R145. Williamson, Susan H. "Review." *Voice of Youth Advocates*, 11 (October 1988): 190.

Favorable review.

The El Dorado Adventure

R146. Andronik, Catherine. "Review." *Book Report*, 6 (March 1988): 33.

Highly recommended. "I have recommended this book to students who love adventure stories; their reviews have been as enthusiastic as mine."

R147. "Review." *Booklist*, 83 (1 April 1987): 1202.

Favorable review.

R148. "Review." *Book Report*, 7 (September 1988): 41.

Highly recommended in a review of the paperback edition of *The El Dorado Adventure*.

R149. "Review." *Catholic Library World*, 59 (March 1988): 230.

"Highly recommended for every library."

R150. "Review." *Childhood Education*, 64 (February 1988): 178.

Favorable review.

R151. Dillon, Brooke. "Review." *Voice of Youth Advocates*, 10 (February 1988): 285.

Favorable review.

R152. Greenlaw, Jean. "Review." *The New Advocate*, 1 (Winter 1988): 74.

Favorable review.

R153. Harding, Susan. "Review." *School Library Journal*, 33 (May 1987): 105.

Starred review. "This book is even more enjoyable than the first. . . . All of the characters, even those who appear only briefly, are well fleshed-out. . . . "

R154. Isaacs, Susan. "Review." *New York Times Book Review*, 7 June 1987, p. 29.

"[W]eakened not only by the predictability of its plot, but by the staleness of its characters . . . . Alexander's prose lacks the texture and power to breathe new life into these familiar [character] types."

R155. Jacobs, James S. "Review." *BYU Children's Book Review*, 7 (May/June 1987): 7.

Favorable review.

R156. "Review." *Kirkus*, 55 (1 March 1987): 369.

Favorable review.

R157. Nix, Kemie. "Review." *Atlanta Journal-Constitution*, 10 April 1986, p. 10J.

Favorable review.

R158. Nix, Kemie. "Review." *Parents' Choice* (Fall/Winter 1987).

Favorable review.

R159. "Review." *Publishers' Weekly*, 231 (13 March 1987): 86.

Favorable review.

R160. "Review." *Reading Teacher*, 41 (October 1987): 99.

Favorable review.

R161. Sutherland, Zena. "Review." *Bulletin of the Center for Children's Books*, 40 (April 1987): 141.

"The wit, the humor, and the doughty protagonist will appeal to readers; the style, the firm characterization, and pointed digs at the foibles of humankind will give them substance."

R162. Twitchell, Ethel R. "Review." *Horn Book*, 63 (May 1987): 344.

"Writing in his usual fast-paced yet carefully crafted style, the author again displays his mastery of the nasty surprise at chapter endings and delivers a rollicking adventure, well stocked with humor."

R163. Tunnell, Michael O. "Review." *Sparks: A Mid-South Children's Book Review Journal*, 1 (Spring 1987): 1.

"[F]ast-paced and carefully plotted. . . . Written in well-crafted and rollicking style, this witty and suspenseful adventure novel takes its rightful place with the other books in the legacy of story given us by Lloyd Alexander."

The First Two Lives of Lukas-Kasha

R164. "Review." *The Best in Children's Books: The University of Chicago Guide to Children's Literature, 1973-1978*. Ed. Zena Sutherland. Chicago: The University of Chicago Press, 1980, pp. 8-9.

Starred review. ". . . a confection of polished style, well-paced plot, and engaging wit."

R165. "Review." *Book World (Washington Post)*(3 December 1978): E4.

"An exceptional fantasy adventure . . ."

R166. "Review." *Bulletin of the Center for Children's Books*, 32 (December 1978): 57.

Starred review. "What gives the story its final high gloss are the depth and nuance of the serious conversation and the transfusion of pithy ideas into the derring-do setting . . . a confection of polished style, well-paced plot, and engaging wit."

R167. Byars, Betsy. "King Kasha and Kim Chu." *Book World (Washington Post)* (12 November 1978): E4.

Boxed review. ". . . an exceptional book, filled with lively dialogue, fun and high adventure. . . . [a] book which makes non-violence attractive and enforces the value of human life has to be taken seriously."

R168. C., L. W. "Review." *Kliatt Young Adult Paperback Book Guide*, 17 (Winter 1983): 16.

"Wrapped in the guise of fantasy, here is a brilliant allegory, bound to delight the pacifists of the world and confound the most calculating of warmongers."

R169. Carver, Kathleen. "Review." *Book Report*, 2 (May 1983): 40.

Highly recommended. "Alexander has succeeded admirably in spinning a tale in time, casting it with memorable characters and enabling the reader to see it on multiple levels."

R170. "Review." *Commonweal*, 105 (10 November 1978): 731.

Favorable review.

R171. Geringer, Laura. "Review." *School Library Journal*, 25 (October 1978): 141.

Starred review. ". . . offers robust, tautly paced adventure, expertly conjured settings, winning heroes, and heroines, a satisfying circular plot, and a few telling twists of fate."

R172. Heins, Paul. "Review." *Horn Book*, 55 (October 1978): 513.

Favorable review.

R173. "Review." *Kirkus*, 46 (15 August 1978): 878.

"Felicitously spun, ingeniously framed adventure."

R174. "Review." *Language Arts*, 56 (April 1979): 444.

"With Lloyd Alexander you usually get something special in the way of a story; this is no exception."

R175. N., J. "Review." *Catholic Library World*, 51 (October 1979): 141.

"This short space does not permit extolling the virtues . . . of this work . . . . The book has humor, marvelously real characters, depth, insight into life and real adventure. . . . It is truly outstanding in every respect. Highly recommended. . . ."

R176. Nix, Kemie. "Review." *The Advocate*, 3 (Fall 1983): 65.

Favorable review.

R177. Nix, Kemie. "Review." *Parents' Choice* (Fall 1980), p. 10.

Favorable review.

R178. Nix, Kemie. "Review." *Atlanta Journal-Constitution*, 22 October 1978, p. 12E.

Favorable review.

R179. Nix, Kemie. "Review." *Atlanta Journal-Constitution*, 10 December 1978, p. 2E.

Favorable review.

R180. "Review." *Publishers' Weekly*, 214 (30 October 1978): 50.

"Having won singular honors for his many books, Alexander is now represented by a fantasy so original, told in such imaginative English, that it may be considered his peak performance."

R181. Sheehan, Ethna. "Review." *America*, 139 (9 December 1978): 442.

Starred review. "Altogether a witty, marvelously plotted, dramatic yarn for ages 11-14."

R182. Sidorsky, Phyllis. "Review." *Childhood Education*, 55 (February 1979): 222.

"This superbly written tale . . . is pure Alexander—amusing, richly detailed, and peopled with intriguing characters."

R183. W., D. M. "Review." *Booklist*, 75 (1 September 1978): 42.

Starred review. ". . . a wonderfully nimble, multilevel fantasy . . . . A most clever, humorous, and soulfully satisfying story."

R184. Wersba, Barbara. *New York Times Book Review*, 10 December 1978, p. 85.

"[Alexander's] newest effort . . . is less than satisfying . . . . One does not enjoy criticizing a writer as good as Lloyd Alexander—but at this point in his career, it might be wise to leave the swashbuckling behind."

Flagship Hope: Aaron Lopez

R185. B., M.W. "Review." *Horn Book*, 37 (April 1961): 163-164.

Favorable review.

R186. "Review." *Booklist*, 57 (15 March 1961): 460.

Favorable review.

R187. "Review." *Kirkus*, 28 (15 August 1960): 685.

Favorable review.

R188. Wennerblad, Sonja. "Review." *Library Journal*, 85 (15 November 1960): 4230.

Favorable review.

The Foundling and Other Tales of Prydain

R189. "Review." *The Best in Children's Books: The University of Chicago Guide to Children's Literature, 1973-1978.* Ed. Zena Sutherland. Chicago: The University of Chicago Press, 1980, p. 9.

"Each tale stands alone, a small gem . . . ."

R190. "Review." *Booklist*, 70 (1 February 1974): 594.

"The characters are striking and the tales lively . . . ."

R191. "Review." *Booklist*, 70 (15 March 1974): 826.

"A gem of a book . . . ."

R192. Fritz, Jean. "Review." *New York Times Book Review*, 4 November 1973, pp. 48, 50.

Favorable review.

R193. Gerhardt, Lillian N. "Review." *Library Journal*, 98 (15 December 1973): 3704.

Favorable review.

R194. H., V. "Review." *Horn Book*, 50 (June 1974): 278.

Favorable review.

R195. "Review." *Kirkus*, 41 (1 December 1973): 1308-1309.

Mixed review. "All worth another hearing as Alexander tells them, but hardly an important contribution to a mythological landscape."

R196. "Review." (Best Books of 1973.) *Library Journal*, 98 (15 December 1973): 3688.

Favorable review.

R197. "Review." *New York Times Book Review*, 4 November 1973, p. 54.

". . . Alexander displays all his skills as he returns to the land of his famous chronicles."

R198. Nix, Kemie. "Review." *Parents' Choice* (Spring 1984), p. 11.

Favorable review.

R199. Nix, Kemie. "Review." *The Advocate*, 2 (Spring 1983): 193.

Favorable review.

R200. "Review." *Publishers' Weekly*, 205 (7 January 1974): 54.

"Some readers will feel a certain disappointment with this book—it's awfully slight—but others will be delighted . . . ."

R201. Sutherland, Zena. "Review." *Bulletin of the Center for Children's Books*, 27 (April 1974): 122.

"Each tale stands alone, a small gem . . . ."

R202. Taylor, Mark. "Review." *Psychology Today*, 7 (May 1974): R20.

Favorable review.

R203. "Review." *Teacher*, 91 (March 1974): 109.

"Knowledge of the earlier books is not necessary to appreciate the skill with which Mr. Alexander uses the short story form or to enjoy the wide range of moods and emotions."

The Four Donkeys

R204. A., E.A. "Review." *Junior Bookshelf*, (April 1975): 94-95+.

"[T]old clearly and concisely but with a zest and attention to detail which well befits this kind of story."

R205. "Review." *Booklist*, 69 (15 February 1973): 571.

"A difficult vocabulary will limit this book to better readers, but its dry wit will appeal to a certain group of young listeners."

R206. "Review." *Growing Point* 41 (May 1975): 2646.

Favorable review.

R207. Fretz, Sada. "Review." *Kirkus*, 40 (15 December 1972): 1407.

Favorable review.

R208. G., J. L. "Review." *Kirkus*, 40 (1 September 1972): 1019.

"Alexander spins this tale with his usual felicity."

R209. McCaul, Isabel. "Review." *Top of the News*, 29 (April 1973): 251.

"Spiked with humor and competently narrated in the style of a folktale . . . ."

R210. McGrew, Mary Lou. "The Book Review." *Library Journal*, 97 (15 December 1972): 4065-4066.

Best Books of 1972. "A tightly constructed, circular story by a master of the modern fanciful tale."

R211. "Review." *New York Times Book Review*, 5 November 1972, p. 47.

"[G]rossly-overblown saga . . . soon degenerates into a peevish shaggy dog story."

R212. Robinson, Beryl. "Review." *Horn Book*, 48 (December 1972): 591.

Favorable review.

R213. Smith, Jennifer Farley.   "Review."   *Christian Science Monitor*, 3
January 1973, p. 6.

"[B]eautifully rendered, marvelous nonsense which few young
children . . . will comprehend—although it may have their parents in
stitches."

R214. Sutherland, Zena.   "Review."   *Bulletin of the Center for Children's
Books*, 26 (March 1973): 101.

Favorable review.

R215. Whalen-Levitt, Peggy. "Review." *School Library Journal*, 32 (March
1986): 101.

Favorable review.

The High King

R216. "Review."   *The Best in Children's Books: The University of Chicago
Guide to Children's Literature, 1966-1972*.   Ed. Zena Sutherland.
Chicago: The University of Chicago Press, 1973, pp. 6-7.

"[T]he grave and pressing matters of the story bring to a poignant finish
the affairs of Taran . . . ."

R217. "Review." *Booklist*, 64 (1 April 1968): 920.

"[D]ramatic and inspiring conclusion to the epic fantasy of Prydain. . . ."

R218. "Review." *Commonweal*, 88 (24 May 1968): 305.

Favorable review.

R219. Fritz, Jean.   "Review."   *New York Times Book Review*, 24 March 1968,
p. 38.

"[O]ne wants to stand up and shout, Bravo!"

R220. Gerhardt, Lillian N. "Review." *Library Journal*, 93 (15 February 1968):
876.

"[T]he strongest high fantasy written for children in our times."

R221. Hamlin, Marjorie D. "Far Back and Far Out." *Christian Science Monitor*, 2 May 1968, p. 38.

"This is imaginative literature at its finest."

R222. Howard, Janet. "Review." *Childhood Education*, 45 (September 1968): 40.

Favorable review.

R223. Kellman, Amy. "Books They'll *Want* to Read This Summer." *Grade Teacher*, 86 (May/June, 1969): 128-129.

"The Newbery-Caldecott Committeemen have paid a deserved tribute to the series as a whole, rather than an individual title."

R224. "Review." *Kirkus*, 36 (1 March 1968): 259.

"The anticlimax should please both the popular philosopher and the sentimentalist . . . ."

R225. Maples, Houston L. "Review." *Book World* (5 May 1968): 22.

"[T]he author has managed to summon the requisite surge of energy and dramatic power to provide so fitting a grand finale."

R226. Miller, Margaret H. "Review." *Top of the News*, 25 (November 1968): 77.

Favorable review.

R227. "Review." *New York Times Book Review*, part 2, 15 February 1970, p. 24.

Favorable review.

R228. Ostermann, Robert. "Review." *National Observer*, 23 September 1968, p. 21.

Favorable review.

R229. "Review." *Publishers' Weekly*, 193 (11 March 1968): 49.

Favorable review.

R230. "Review." *Publishers' Weekly*, 218 (26 September 1980): 122.

"Admirers of Alexander [were] 'both glad and sad that he has written the finale to his Chronicles of Prydain.' The five books were praised for style, depth and mysticism as well as for thrilling episodes . . . ."

R231. Rooney, Eugene M. "Review." *Best Sellers*, 28 (1 May 1968): 62.

Favorable review.

R232. S., S.M.E. "Review." *Catholic Library World*, 41 (October 1969): 140.

"[A]n exceptionally fine combination of fantasy, humor and a tremendous display of heroism on the part of the well defined characters."

R233. "Review." *Saturday Review*, 51 (20 April 1968): 41.

"The fantasy has the depth and richness of a medieval tapestry, infinitely detailed and imaginative."

R234. Sutherland, Zena. "Review." *Bulletin of the Center for Children's Books*, 21 (May 1968): 137.

"Although there is humor here, the grave and pressing matters of the story bring to a poignant finish the affairs of Taran and his circle . . . ."

R235. V., R.H. "Review." *Horn Book*, 44 (April 1968): 171-172.

"More than a series of exciting adventures, the book has the philosophical depth and overtones of great fantasy."

R236. "Review." *Young Reader's Review*, 4 (April 1968): 13.

"There are few books which are so truly heroic in concept, poetic and haunting in imagery, so filled with great and continually growing characters."

The Illyrian Adventure

R237. "Review." *Booklist*, 86 (1 January 1990): 923.

Favorable review.

R238. Bradurn, Frances. "Review." *Wilson Library Bulletin*, 62 (January 1987): 61.

Favorable review.

R239. "Review." *Bulletin of the Center for Children's Books*, 39 (April 1986): 142.

Favorable review.

R240. Burns, Mary M. *Horn Book*, 62 (July 1986): 447.

"Lloyd Alexander has a positive genius for creating imaginary kingdoms. . . . What makes his work truly excellent . . . is his strong sense of story, controlled but not dominated by a substantial theme, and his ability to meld the actual and the imagined into a plausible reality."

R241. Chamberlin, Leslie. *Voice of Youth Advocates*, 9 (December 1986): 232.

Favorable review.

R242. "Review." *Childhood Education*, 63 (December 1986): 30.

Favorable review.

R243. "Review." *Children's Book Review Service*, 14 (June 1986): 123.

Favorable review.

R244. Clark, Hattie. "Review." *Christian Science Monitor*, 3 July 1986, p. B6.

"The book shows considerable craft, with every word doing full duty. And as usual, Alexander doesn't patronize in the areas of vocabulary and intellectual references."

R245. Harper, Susan H. "Review." *Fantasy Review*, 9 (September 1986): 33.

"Alexander's books are already favorites with young adults and this new entry can only increase that reputation. Vesper does not merely live on the page, she tears across it. . . . Readers had better run to get this book . . . ."

R246. Jacobs, James S. "Review." *BYU Children's Book Review*, 6 (May/June 1986): 5.

Favorable review.

R247. "Review." *Kirkus*, 54 (1 April 1986): 543.

Favorable review.

R248. "Review." *Magazine of Fantasy and Science Fiction*, 73 (October 1987): 35.

"It is the stuff that dreams are made of. I wish I had had this book when I was twelve. I was delighted to read it even now when I'm old."

R249. McKee, Barbara J. "Review." *Book Report*, 6 (May 1987): 40.

Favorable review.

R250. Miller, Sara. "Review." *School Library Journal*, 32 (May 1986): 99.

Favorable review.

R251. Nix, Kemie. "Review." *Atlanta Journal-Constitution*, 6 July 1986, p. 10J.

Favorable review.

R252. Nix, Kemie. *Parents' Choice*, 9 (Fall/Winter 1986), p. 27.

Favorable review.

R253. "Review." *Publishers' Weekly*, 229 (30 May 1986): 67.

Favorable review.

R254. "Review." *Reading Teacher*, 40 (October 1986): 92.

Favorable review.

R255. "Review." *Reading Teacher*, 41 (October 1987): 51.

Favorable review.

R256. Rusk, Sue. "Review." *Book Report*, 5 (November 1986): 26.

Favorable review.

R257. Shanahan, Michael. "Review." *Best Sellers*, 46 (June 1986): 115.

Lloyd Alexander's latest novel is a winner. *The Illyrian Adventure* has everything a young person looks for in a book . . . ."

R258. W., D. M. "Review." *Booklist*, 82 (1 April 1986): 1137.

Starred review. "A lively yarn from this veteran teller of robust tales."

R259. W., S. H. "Review." *Kliatt Young Adult Paperback Book Guide*, 21 (Spring 1987): 19.

"This is an absolutely charming tale; Vesper is a wonderful heroine, and the prose exceptionally witty."

The Jedera Adventure

R260. Britsch, Barbara. "Review." *Perspectives*, 6 (Spring 1990): 39.

"Crisp writing, vivid descriptions . . . . Unlike some sequels, each Vesper Holly adventure is as captivating as previous ones, and leaves us longing for more."

R261. Del Negro, Janice M. "Review." *School Library Journal*, 35 (May 1989): 124.

Favorable review.

R262. Dillon, Brooke. "Review." *Voice of Youth Advocates*, 12 (August 1989): 162.

"The high level of vocabulary and sophisticated sentence construction will appeal to both teachers and parents, and make the book a very effective one for reading aloud. *The Jedera Adventure* is another delightful Alexander creation."

R263. Hearne, Betsy. "Review." *Bulletin of the Center for Children's Books*, 42 (June 1989): 242.

Favorable review.

R264. Heins, Ethel L. "Review." *Horn Book*, 65 (September/October 1989): 624-625.

"Once again the novel is dominated by the incomparable intelligence, idealism, courage, and charm of the protagonist, and, as before, the hyperbolic aspects of the story are counterbalanced by the elegant, witty, beautifully paced writing."

R265. "Review." *Kirkus*, 57 (1 April 1989): 543.

"Once again, Alexander works his magic . . . . Fine, comic high adventure . . . ."

R266. M., S. A. "Review." *Children's Book Review Service*, 17 (July 1989): 147.

"[D]elightful entertainment for young teens."

R267. Nix, Kemie. "Review." *Atlanta Journal-Constitution*, 30 April 1989, p. 11N.

Favorable review.

R268. "Review." *Publishers' Weekly*, 235 (24 February 1989): 234.

"Once again, the author succeeds in combining impeccably paced adventure with thoughtful, compassionate evocation of a foreign land."

R269. Rochman, Hazel. "Review." *Booklist*, 85 (1 June 1989): 1717.

Favorable review.

R270. Whitmore, Tom. "Review." *Locus*, 23 (August 1989): 19, 56.

"It's a pleasant naive romp, filled with ideas that will make you wince if you think about them (the depictions of tribesman are Kiplingesque in their simple racism) but quite a bit of fun if you don't think."

R271. Wilms, Denise. "Review." *Booklist*, 85 (1 June 1989): 1718.

Favorable review.

The Kestrel

R272. "Review." *The Best in Children's Books: The University of Chicago Guide to Children's Literature, 1979-1984.* Ed. Zena Sutherland. Chicago: The University of Chicago Press, 1986, p. 10.

Starred review. "Another smasher."

R273. "Review." *Booklist*, 81 (15 December 1984): 583.

Favorable review.

R274. "Review." *Booklist*, 83 (15 April 1987): 1299.

Favorable review.

R275. "Review." *Bulletin of the Center for Children's Books*, 35 (June 1982): 181.

Starred review. "In a sequel to *Westmark* Alexander moves . . . to deeper issues and subtler levels. . . . Another smasher."

R276. "Review." *Catholic Library World*, 54 (March 1983): 333.

"While Alexander has presented a vivid, biting portrait of the evils of war . . . he has nevertheless presented a novel of depth and action with most memorable characters. . . . A superior book for grades 5 and up."

R277. "Review." *Children's Book Review Service*, 10 (May 1982): 95.

Favorable review.

R278. D. M. "Review." *Booklist*, 78 (15 April 1982): 1091.

Starred review. "Readers of *Westmark* will welcome this brimming continuation of the story . . . . The tale is an ambitious one, more complex than its predecessor, but ultimately no less satisfying."

R279. Gardner, Craig Shaw. "Fantasy to Cut Your Teeth On." *Book World* (*Washington Post*), 13 (9 January 1983): 11.

Favorable review.

R280. Heins, Paul. "Review." *Horn Book*, 58 (August 1982): 410.

Favorable review.

R281. "Review." *Horn Book*, 60 (February 1984): 84.

Favorable review.

R282. J., C. "Review." *Social Education*, 47 (April 1983): 249.

"The rich characterizations and well-constructed plot and subplot keep this chronicle of ageless conflicts and concerns rolling right along."

R283. "Review." *Journal of Reading*, 26 (October 1982): 87.

"*The Kestrel* is sure to be an award winner, too."

R284. "Review." *Kirkus*, 50 (1 April 1982): 417.

"This is old-fashioned story-telling through-and-through, its handling of themes more fossilized than timeless—which is probably fine with Alexander's audience."

R285. "Review." *Kliatt Young Adult Paperback Book Guide*, 18 (Winter 1984): 21.

Favorable review.

R286. Klopp, Eleanor. "Review." *Voice of Youth Advocates*, 5 (October 1982): 48.

Favorable review.

R287. "Review." *Language Arts*, 60 (March 1983): 361.

Favorable review.

R288. McHargue, Georgess. "Review." *New York Times Book Review*, 25 April 1982, p. 47.

"The story loses its vitality because Alexander seems determined to make issues come before character, language, atmosphere or even emotion."

R289. Moore, Teresa. "Area Booksellers Name Their Favorite Titles." *Book World (Washington Post)*, 18 (8 May 1988): 16-17.

Favorable review.

R290. "Review." *New York Times Book Review*, 5 February 1984, p. 34.

Favorable review.

R291. Nix, Kemie. "Review." *The Advocate*, 3 (Spring 1984): 208.

Favorable review.

R292. Nix, Kemie. "Review." *Atlanta Journal-Constitution*, 6 June 1982, p. 10H.

Favorable review.

R293. Nix, Kemie. "Review." *Parents' Choice* (Fall/Winter 1982).

Favorable review.

R294. Nix, Kemie. "Review." *Parents' Choice* (Spring/Summer 1984), p. 2.

Favorable review.

R295. Perlick, Mary Alaine. "Review." *Best Sellers*, 42 (October 1982): 284.

Favorable review.

R296. "Review." *Publishers' Weekly*, 221 (14 May 1982): 216.

Favorable review.

R297. Rochman, Hazel. "Review." *School Library Journal*, 28 (April 1982): 64.

Starred review. "The fast-paced plot, subtleties of character, ironic wit, quiet understatement and pervasive animal imagery—all work with superb concentration to undercut the heroics of war."

The King's Fountain

R298. B., C. J. "Review." *Catholic Library World*, 43 (November 1971): 173.

Favorable review.

R299. "Review." *Booklist*, 68 (1 September 1971): 55.

Favorable review.

R300. Farrell, Diane. "Review." *New York Times Book Review*, 25 July 1971, p. 8.

"[E]laborately contrived, didactic framework confuses the issues, dulls the impact and obscures the lesson."

R301. Gerhardt, Lillian N. "Review." (Best Books for Spring, 1971). *Library Journal*, 96 (15 May 1971): 1780.

"A rare book to trigger thought and delight the eye."

R302. Gerhardt, Lillian N., Diane G. Stavn and Pamela D. Pollack. "Review." (Best Books of 1971). *Library Journal*, 96 (15 December 1971): 4157.

Favorable review.

R303. "Review." *Grade Teacher*, 89 (November 1971): 88.

Favorable review.

R304. Heins, Paul. "Review." *Horn Book*, 47 (August 1971): 373.

"The telling is casual rather than pointed, and misses the precision of a true parable."

R305. "Review." *Kirkus*, 39 (15 February 1971): 167.

"The result is both overwhelming and uninviting."

R306. "Review." *Publishers' Weekly*, 69 (24 May 1971): 69.

"Lloyd Alexander has never written with a cleaner pen."

R307. Sheehan, Ethna. "Children's Books at Christmastime." *America*, (4 December 1971): 486.

Favorable review.

R308. "Review." *Social Studies*, 77 (November 1986): 235.

Favorable review.

R309. Stavn, Diane G. "Review." *Library Journal*, 96 (15 June 1971): 2124.

Favorable review.

R310. Sutherland, Zena. "On the Road." *Saturday Review*, 54 (19 June 1971): 26

Favorable review.

R311. Sutherland, Zena. "Review." *Bulletin of the Center for Children's Books*, 24 (July/August 1971): 165.

"The writing has a stately quality, some of it difficult . . . but the plot is not complex and the theme is made clear."

R312. Wentroth, Mary Ann. "Recent Children's Books." *Top of the News*, 28 (November 1971): 73.

Favorable review.

The Marvelous Misadventures of Sebastian

R313. B., C.J. "Review." *Catholic Library World*, 43 (November 1971): 174.

Favorable review.

R314. "Review." *The Best in Children's Books: The University of Chicago Guide to Children's Literature, 1966-1972.* Ed. Zena Sutherland. Chicago: The University of Chicago Press, 1973, p. 7.

"The intricacy of plot, the humor and allusiveness of the writing, the exaggerated characterization, and the derring-do of romantic adventures are knit into a lively and elaborate tale . . . ."

R315. "Review." *Booklist*, 67 (15 November 1970): 266.

"The story has an intriguing cast of characters and exhibits the author's flair for wit and irony."

R316. "Review." *Booklist*, 67 (1 April 1971): 659.

Favorable review.

R317. "Review." *Book World*, part 2 (13 May 1973): 7.

Favorable review.

R318. Dorsey, Margaret A. "Review." *Library Journal*, 95 (15 November 1970): 4040.

". . . Mr. Alexander writes a jolly good story and still manages to provide his readers with plenty of food for thought."

R319. G., L.N. "Review." (Best Books of 1970). *Library Journal*, 95 (15 December 1970); 4324.

"Most amusing high adventure . . . ."

R320. "Review." *Grade Teacher*, 87 (April 1971): 26-27.

Favorable review.

R321. Harrington, Roseanne H. "Books for Children." *Childhood Education*, 47 (May 1971): 437.

"Told in the mood of comic opera, the story fairly gallops along . . . ."

R322. Heins, Paul. "Review." *Horn Book*, 46 (December 1970): 628.

"The story is a comic fantasy, successfully combining eighteenth-century briskness with romantic moonshine."

R323. Maples, Houston L. "Review." *Book World*, 4, part 2 (8 November 1970): 10.

"This is effortless entertainment from an author who knows how to please and obviously enjoys himself at the same time."

R324. "Review." *Publishers' Weekly*, 198 (2 November 1970): 53.

Favorable review.

R325. "Review." *Saturday Review*, 54 (23 January 1971): 71.

"[T]he articulate and vivid writing pulls together the threads of picaresque action, humor, chicanery, social commentary, and romance into an intricate and lively whole."

R326. Sutherland, Zena. "Review." *Bulletin of the Center for Children's Books*, 24 (February 1971): 85-86.

"[A] lively and elaborate tale that can be enjoyed and appreciated for its subtler significance."

R327. Wersba, Barbara. "Review." *New York Times Book Review*, 15 November 1970, p. 42.

"[Alexander] knows how to write characters in a way that can touch the heart."

The Philadelphia Adventure

R328. Behrmann, Christine. "Review." *School Library Journal*, 36 (March 1990): 215-216.

"[E]ccentrically entertaining characterizations, seamless plotting, and breakneck pace."

R329. P., K. "Review." *Bulletin of the Center for Children's Books*, 43 (March 1990): 152.

"The combination of historical fact, non-stop danger and intrigue, and masterful writing style adds up to another energetic predicament for Vesper Holly."

R330. "Review." *The Horn Book*, 66 (March/April 1990): 225.

Favorable review.

R331. "Review." *Kirkus*, 58 (March 15, 1990): 420.

Pointer (starred review). "Alexander provides a note to distinguish historical fact from his clever fictions. Vastly entertaining."

R332. Wilms, Denise. "Review." *Booklist*, 86 (March 1, 1990): 1337.

"The action is quick and the characterizations bright and bold. There are no forced movements here: this tale moves easily from start to finish . . . ."

Prydain Chronicles **(Reviews of the Prydain series rather than of the individual books)**

R333. "Review." *English Journal*, 69 (October 1980): 72.

Favorable review.

Taran Wanderer

R334. "Review." *The Best in Children's Books: The University of Chicago Guide to Children's Literature, 1966-1972*. Ed. Zena Sutherland. Chicago: The University of Chicago Press, 1973, p. 7.

"[T]here is, in fact, all the color and adventure one expects in the land of fantasy."

R335. "Review." *Best Sellers*, 27 (1 May 1967): 63.

Favorable review.

R336. "Review." *Booklist*, 63 (15 April 1967): 905.

"this pointed and spirited [book] . . . has more depth than the earlier stories."

R337. Fritz, Jean. "Review." *New York Times Book Review*, 9 April 1967, p. 26.

"[W]hile his plots follow a slashing heroic pattern, his quest is into the subtleties of manhood itself."

R338. Gerhardt, Lillian N. "Review." *Library Journal*, 92 (15 May 1967): 2025.

"This is an independent title in the strongest fantasy series being created for children in our time."

R339. King, Martha Bennett. "Review." *Books Today* (Chicago Tribune), 7 May 1967, p. 18A.

"[A]esthetically complete without the other books . . . ."

R340. "Review." *Kirkus*, 35 (15 February 1967): 195.

"Mr. Alexander has constructed a remarkable panorama of humor, terror, and high adventure."

R341. Maples, Houston L. "Making Belief." *Bookweek* (7 May 1967): 6.

Favorable review.

R342. "Review." *New York Times Book Review*, 5 November 1967, p. 66.

Favorable review.

R343. Omdal, Marsha De Prez. "For Wayfarers Still Journeying." *Language Arts*, 55 (April 1978): 501-502.

"[A]n excellent choice for study by junior high school literature classes. Through noble and dramatic language Lloyd Alexander presents a character whose emotions relate directly to those of a young person. This is a unique type of fantasy."

R344. "Review." *Publishers' Weekly*, 191 (10 April 1967): 81.

Favorable review.

R345. "Review." *Saturday Review*, 50 (18 March 1967): 36.

"The story has a nice balance of humor and poignant sadness."

R346. Sutherland, Zena. "Review." *Bulletin of the Center for Children's Books*, 20 (May 1967): 133.

"A bit more somber than the preceding books, this is also more significant; although the theme is serious, there is no paucity of daring forays, wicked enchanters, tiny people, desperate fights, et cetera . . . ."

R347. V., R.H. "Review." *Horn Book*, 43 (June 1967): 341.

"[T]he mature, thoughtful ending is very satisfying."

R348. Way, Olivia R. "Review." *Instructor*, 67 (May 1967): 132.

Favorable review.

R349. "Review." *Young Reader's Review*, 3 (June 1967): 12.

"This is a wise and noble book, learned with the same humor that the other three boasted."

Time Cat

R350. Buell, Ellen Lewis. "Young Reader's Shelf: A Selection from Recent Titles." *New York Times Book Review*, 14 April 1963, p. 56.

"Filled with excitement and humor . . . ."

R351. Libby, Margaret Sherwood. "Review." *New York Herald Tribune Book Review*, Section 12, 12 May 1963, p. 5.

Favorable review.

R352. "Review." *London Times Literary Supplement*, 28 November 1963, p. 980.

Unfavorable review.

R353. Lux, Louise. "Review." *Philadelphia Bulletin*, 18 April 1963.

Favorable review.

R354. Mathes, Miriam S. "Review." *Library Journal*, 88 (15 June 1963): 2548.

"[E]pisodic treatment fails to sustain excitement throughout, but this will appeal to good readers who enjoy an occasional fresh, humorous insight into history."

R355. "Review." *New Statesman*, (8 November 1963): 668.

"Clear-cut style. No nonsense."

R356. "Review." *Publishers' Weekly*, 194 (22 July 1967): 67.

Favorable review.

R357. "Review." *Saturday Review*, 46 (11 May 1963): 49.

Favorable review.

The Town Cats and Other Tales

R358. "Review." *The Best in Children's Books: The University of Chicago Guide to Children's Literature, 1973-1978.* Ed. Zena Sutherland. Chicago: The University of Chicago Press, 1980, p. 9.

Starred review. "Alexander at his best."

R359. Eby, Eleanor. "Alexander the Great." *Philadelphia Inquirer*, 26 February 1978, p. 11-I.

"It is one of the finest books he has written, and one of the most *fun* books . . . . And then, each of Alexander's eight stories is more delightful than the one preceding it."

R360. Flowers, Ann A. "Review." *Horn Book*, 54 (February 1978): 42.

"The author is well known for his esteem and affection for cats, and there are few writers better qualified to give them their due. An excellent collection for reading or storytelling . . . "

R361. Fritz, Jean. "Six by Winners." *New York Times Book Review*, 13 November 1977, p. 63.

"The language is delicious and the moral is clear. We should pay more attention to cats, especially to Lloyd Alexander's cats."

R362. "Review." *Kirkus*, 45 (15 October 1977): 1096.

"Eight fanciful, sparkling fairy tales . . . ."

R363. L., E. "Review." *Children's Book Review Service* (January 1978): 42.

Favorable review.

R364. Miller, Sara. "Review." *School Library Journal*, 24 (November 1977): 52.

Favorable review.

R365. "Review." *New York Times Book Review*, 24 May 1981, p. 19.

Favorable review.

R366. Nix, Kemie. "Some Funny Lines on Felines." *Atlanta Journal-Constitution*, 25 December 1977, p. 22C.

Favorable review.

R367. Sutherland, Zena. *Bulletin of the Center for Children's Books*, 31 (February 1978): 89.

Starred review. ". . . fresh, witty, and written in polished, deceptively light style; beneath the magic and humor and entertaining dialogue are perceptive insights into the foibles of creatures, feline or human . . . . Alexander at his best."

R368. "Review." *Teacher*, 95 (October 1977): 154.

Favorable review.

R369. W., D. M. "Review." *Booklist*, 74 (1 November 1977): 472.

Starred review. "There's great style to these cat stories in the fairy tale mode. Alexander is a master of the form and his language flows easily, effortlessly. . . . Eight stories in all, each worth savoring—a treasure cache."

The Truthful Harp

R370. Beatty, Jr., Jerome. "Review." *New York Times Book Review*, part 2, 5 November 1967, p. 63.

Favorable review.

R371. "Review." *The Best in Children's Books: The University of Chicago Guide to Children's Literature, 1966-1972*. Ed. Zena Sutherland. Chicago: The University of Chicago Press, 1973, p. 7.

"[T]he writing has humor, vitality, and a distinctive turn of phrase."

R372. "Review." *Commonweal*, 87 (10 November 1967): 178.

Favorable review.

R373. Gerhardt, Lillian N. "Review." *Library Journal*, 92 (15 December 1967): 4608.

"[C]an stand alone as one of the very few amusing stories for younger children about growth and self-discipline."

R374. H., E.L. "Review." *Horn Book*, 44 (February 1968): 58.

Favorable review.

R375. King, Martha Bennett. "Review." *Book World* (26 November 1967): 16.

"[O]utstanding for originality in both story and illustrations."

R376. "Review." *Kirkus*, 35 (15 October 1967): 1268.

"The interplay of courtliness and wit is consistent throughout the tight story . . . ."

R377. "Review." *National Observer*, 27 November 1967, p. 21.

Favorable review.

R378. Nordell, Roderick. "Review." *Christian Science Monitor*, 2 November 1967, p. B2.

Favorable review.

R379. "Review." *Publishers' Weekly*, 192 (20 November 1967): 56.

"[Y]our reviewer is not one whom Lloyd Alexander had enthralled— until *The Truthful Harp*."

R380. "Review." *Saturday Review*, 50 (27 January 1967): 35.

"The style is distinctive, the character engaging, the humor light . . . ."

R381. Sutherland, Zena. "Review." *Bulletin of the Center for Children's Books*, 21 (February 1968): 89.

"[T]he writing has humor, vitality, and a distinctive turn of phrase."

Westmark

R382. "Review." *The Best in Children's Books: The University of Chicago Guide to Children's Literature, 1979-1984*. Ed. Zena Sutherland. Chicago: The University of Chicago Press, 1986, pp. 10-11.

Starred review. "A superb craftsman, Alexander has concocted a marvelous tale of high adventure . . . ."

R383. Bolley, Jean S. "Review." *Voice of Youth Advocates*, 4 (October 1981): 41.

Favorable review.

R384. "Review." *Book Report*, 1 (March 1983): 23.

Favorable review.

R385. "Review." *Book World (Washington Post)*, 12 (11 July 1982): 12.

Favorable review.

R386. "Review." *Bulletin of the Center for Children's Books*, 34 (June 1981): 195.

Starred review. "A superb craftsman, Alexander has concocted a marvelous tale of high adventure . . . . Lloyd Alexander is a master of writing dialogue, of blending many facets and plot threads into a smooth whole, and above all of conceiving characters with depth and conviction."

R387. "Review." *Children's Book Review Service*, 9 (May 1981): 85.

"The one-dimensional characters are compensated for by the satisfying story, typically Alexander in its irony, wryness, and vitality."

R388. D., D. C. "Review." *Kliatt Young Adult Paperback Book Guide*, 16 (Fall 1982): 4.

". . . *Westmark* is a cut above the usual leisure piece in that its characters are not mere shallow representations of good and evil . . . . *Westmark* uses subtle twists and turns of plot to interplay politics with personalities making for an exciting, thought-provoking tale."

R389. E., B. "Review." *Booklist*, 77 (1 April 1981): 1095.

Starred review. "As usual, Alexander peoples his tale with a marvelous cast of individuals, and weaves an intricate story of high adventure that climaxes in a superbly conceived conclusion . . . ."

R390. Elleman, Barbara. "Review." *Learning*, 13 (April 1985): 28.

Favorable review.

R391. Fritz, Jean. "Review." *New York Times Book Review*, 10 May 1981, p. 38.

"Lloyd Alexander . . . [has perfected] the art of storytelling and becoming ever more wise in the ways of humankind. . . . The wisdom of [this] book lies in its difficult solution: good does not triumph over evil simply because it *is* good."

R392. G., M. J. "Review." *Journal of Reading*, 25 (December 1981): 288.

"[A]n exciting and adventurous story replete with the marvelous facility for language that Alexander always exhibits."

R393. H., J. "Review." *Catholic Library World*, 53 (September 1981): 90.

Highly recommended. "A short review can in no way do justice to this splendid novel. Lloyd Alexander is truly at his best here creating vivid characters, high paced adventure, much humor and a philosophical outlook of life truly deserving to be read by students grades 5 and up."

R394. Heins, Ethel L. "Review." *Horn Book*, 57 (August 1981): 428.

"The author's most inventive book in years is both a picaresque novel and an energetic cloak-and-dagger tale with a climax as breathtaking as that of a Douglas Fairbanks film. . . . Adroitly the author maneuvers the crisscrossing threads of his complex, but brilliantly controlled, plot . . . ."

R395. "Review." *Instructor*, 92 (September 1982): 20.

Favorable review.

R396. "Review." *Kirkus* 49 (August 1981): 934.

Favorable review.

R397. "Review." *Language Arts*, 58 (October 1981): 847.

"[A]mong Alexander's finest . . . . a *tour de force* . . . . A book to hug to one's heart."

R398. Manning, Patricia. "Review." *School Library Journal*, 27 (May 1981): 62.

Starred review. "Rich language, excellent characterization, detailed descriptions and a dovetailed plot equal superb craftsmanship. Alexander has done it again."

R399. Moore, Teresa. "Area Booksellers Names Their Favorite Titles." *Book World (Washington Post)*, 18 (8 May 1988): 16-17.

Favorable review.

R400. "Review." *New York Times Book Review*, 9 January 1983, p. 39.

Favorable review.

R401. Nix, Kemie. "Review." *The Advocate*, 3 (Winter 1984): 139.

Favorable review.

R402. Nix, Kemie. "Review." *Atlanta Journal-Constitution*, 24 May 1981, p. 11E.

Favorable review.

R403. Nix, Kemie. "Review." *Parents' Choice* (Winter 1981), p. 11.

Favorable review.

R404. Nix, Kemie. "Review." *Parents' Choice* (Fall 1981), p. 8.

Favorable review.

R405. "Review." *Reading Teacher*, 35 (January 1982): 499.

Favorable review.

R406. Roedder, Kathleen. "Review." *Childhood Education*, 58 (November 1981): 108.

Favorable review.

R407. "Review." *Voice of Youth Advocates*, 5 (February 1983): 60.

Favorable review.

The Wizard in the Tree

R408. "Review." *America: National Catholic Weekly Review*, 133, 6 December 1975, p. 403.

"Clever, witty dialogue and swift action, with originality of characterization . . . ."

R409. "Review." *The Best in Children's Books: The University of Chicago Guide to Children's Literature, 1973-1978*. Ed. Zena Sutherland. Chicago: The University of Chicago Press, 1980, pp. 9-10.

"[T]he writing is vigorous and the characterization sly, the plot an inventive embroidery of the battle between good and evil."

R410. "Review." *Booklist*, 71 (1 April 1975): 813.

Favorable review.

R411. Burns, Mary M. "Review." *Horn Book*, 51 (August 1975): 377, 379.

"Favorable review.

R412. "Review." *Catholic Library World*, 47 (October 1975): 132.

Favorable review.

R413. "Review." *Kirkus*, 43 (15 April 1975): 451.

"[Q]uick-witted melodrama and nimble-tongued romanticism."

R414. Lewis, Marjorie. "Review." *School Library Journal*, 21 (May 1975): 45.

Favorable review.

R415. M., R.E. "Review." *Language Arts*, 52 (November 1975): 1165.

Alexander's talents are again evident in brisk dialogue, exciting plot, and unusual but believable characters."

R416. Sutherland, Zena. "Review." *Bulletin of the Center for Children's Books*, 28 (July/August 1975): 173.

"[T]he writing is vigorous and the characterization sly, the plot an inventive embroidery of the battle between good and evil."

R417. Wersba, Barbara. "Review." *New York Times Book Review*, 4 May 1975, p. 34.

"If [Alexander] is to continue as an artist, he must find new countries to explore."

a. Translations

Nausea by Jean-Paul Sartre

R418. Nabokov, Vladimir. "Sartre's First Try." *New York Times Book Review*, 24 April 1949, p. 3, 9.

"Lack of space limits me to only these examples of Mr. Alexander's blunders." Nabokov then lists three mistakes. He concludes: "But the task to make the world exist as a work of art was beyond Sartre's powers."

Selected Writings of Paul Eluard

R419. Deutsch, Babette. "In Verse Paul Eluard Speaks of the Love for Mankind." *New York Times Book Review*, 21 October 1951, p. 24.

"Unfortunately, the translation fails to convey the purity of the originals, the sonorities of the verse, the skillful management of cadence, the witty ambiguities, nor is it always faithful to the sense of the text."

5. Audio-Visual Media Relating to Lloyd Alexander

AV 1. "The Black Cauldron." Animated feature film. Walt Disney Productions, 1985.

AV 2. "The Black Cauldron Machine-readable Data File." Computer software (six program files on 5 1/4 inch disks, IBM or Tandy 1000; 1 booklet; 1 reference card; 1 map). Walt Disney Personal Computer Software, Sierra On-Line, Inc., 1985.

AV 3. "The Cat Who Wished to Be a Man." Shiki Theatrical Company, Japan, May 1 through Oct. 31, 1989.

AV 4. Durell, Ann. "Interview with Lloyd Alexander," supplemental cassette tape for basal reader, *Riders of the Earth*. New York: Holt, Rinehart and Winston, 1974.

AV 5. "Enjoying Poetry with Children." Spoken recording. Children's Book Council, 1976.

AV 6. "Fantasy and the Human Condition." Mini-seminars, cassette tape, *Prelude II*. Children's Book Council, 1977.

AV 7. Glassner, Sherwin, Edward Grossman, and Mary McCay. "Sunburst Reading Skillbuilders." Media kit. Sunburst Communications, 1976.

AV 8. "The High King." Filmstrips and cassettes. Miller Brody/Random House, 1974.

AV 9. "I Want to Know More about Good Books II." Media Kit. Sunburst Communications, 1981.

AV10. "Lloyd Alexander, Evaline Ness, and Ann Durell." Videorecording. Temple University, Dept. of Educational Media, 1974.

AV11. "Meet the Newbery Author Filmstrip Series: Lloyd Alexander." Filmstrip and cassette. New York: Miller Brody/Random House, 1974.

AV12. Potter, Alene. "Meet the Author: Lloyd Alexander." Spoken recording. Imperial International Learning, 1969.

AV13. "Seeing with the Third Eye." Spoken recording. National Council of Teachers of English, 1973.

AV14. "Selected Readings." Spoken recording. Connecticut Films, Inc., 1979.

AV15. "Will There Be Children after 1984?" Spoken recording. Convention Recording Services, 1984.

AV16. *"The Wizard in the Tree, The Marvelous Misadventures of Sebastian, My Five Tigers, The Cat Who Wished to be a Man.* Selected Readings." Spoken recording. Dutton, 1975.

6. Miscellaneous Sources

M 1. Arbuthnot, May Hill. *Children's Reading in the Home.* Glenview, Illinois: Scott, Foresman, 1969, pp. 161-162.

A brief introduction to Lloyd Alexander, giving him credit for being the first American to write "British" high fantasy. She also summarizes *The Book of Three.*

M 2. Bisenieks, Dainis. "Children, Magic, and Choices." *Mythlore,* 6 (Winter 1979): 13-16.

In this discussion of the merits of different works of fantasy, Alexander comes off well as the creator of believable characters and situations which teach indirectly, and therefore powerfully, without giving in to moralizing.

M 3. Boyer, Robert H., and Kenneth J. Zahorski, eds. "Lloyd Alexander." In *The Fantastic Imagination.* New York: Avon, 1977, pp. 263-64.

The authors present a brief biographical sketch of Alexander that precedes a reprinting of "The Foundling."

M 4. Boyer, Robert H., and Kenneth J. Zahorski, eds. "Lloyd Alexander." In *The Fantastic Imagination II.* New York: Avon, 1978, pp. 249-251.

The authors present a brief biographical sketch of Alexander that precedes a reprinting of "The Weaver, the Smith, and the Harper."

M 5. Carter, Lin. *Imaginary Worlds: The Art of Fantasy*. New York: Ballantine, 1973, pp. 128-130.

Carter praises Alexander for his craftsmanship and character development in Prydain. He also alludes to the humor. "Another thing that makes the series stand out in my mind is the unexpected element of humor that enlivens every page. This, once again, is the mark of intelligence: the tension is taut throughout, and unrelieved, it would have been harrowing."

M 6. Fisher, Margery. *Who's Who in Children's Books?* London: Weldenfeld and Nicholson, 1975.

The author adds a brief biographical piece on Alexander in this collective biography about children's writers.

M 7. Kingman, Lee. *Newbery and Caldecott Medal Books: 1966-1975*. Boston: Horn Book, 1975, pp. 162-163, 174-176.

Detailed plot outlines for *The High King* and *The Black Cauldron*.

M 8. Polette, Nancy. "Lloyd Alexander." In *A Treasury of Letters from Favorite Authors*. By Nancy Polette. O'Fallon, Missouri: Book Lures, 1979, pp. 1-3.

Polette gives a brief biographical sketch of Lloyd Alexander that precedes an open letter Alexander has written to his young readers.

M 9. Townsend, John Rowe. *Written for Children*. 3rd rev. ed. New York: Lippincott, 1987, pp. 240-242.

Crediting only a few American writers with the ability to write fantasy, Townsend begrudgingly gives Alexander credit for being one who has to some degree been successful. He allows Alexander respect for having in Prydain "conceived and carried out a large, complex design" though without "catching the true spirit either of Wales or of Welsh legend."

M10. Waggoner, Diana. "Lloyd Alexander." In *The Hills of Faraway: A Guide to Fantasy*. New York: Atheneum, 1978, pp. 128-129.

The author includes a brief biographical sketch of Lloyd Alexander.

M11. Walt Disney Pictures. *Walt Disney Pictures' The Black Cauldron*. New York: Scholastic, 1985.

This Disney picture book is loosely based on the book by Lloyd Alexander.

M12. Walt Disney Pictures. *The Black Cauldron: Taran and the Fairfolk.* New York: Golden Book, 1985.

This Disney picture book is loosely based on the book by Lloyd Alexander.

M13. Walt Disney Pictures. *Walt Disney's The Black Cauldron: Taran's Magic Sword.* Bristol: Purnell, 1985.

This Disney picture book is loosely based on the book by Lloyd Alexander.

M14. Weber, Rosemary. "Lloyd Alexander." In *Twentieth-Century Children's Writers.* Ed. D. L. Kirkpatrick. New York: St. Martin's Press, 1983, pp. 20-22.

This is a brief biographical entry about Lloyd Alexander which includes critical analysis of some of his works.

APPENDIX I:
AWARDS

The Black Cauldron

The John Newbery Honor Medal, 1966.

Border Hawk: August Bondi

The National Jewish Book Award, 1959.

The Cat Who Wished to be Man

Boston Globe-Horn Book Honors for Fiction, 1973.

The First Two Lives of Lukas-Kasha

National Book Award Finalist, 1979.
CRABbery Award (Prince George's County Memorial Library System, Oxon Hill, MD), 1979.
The Dutch "Silver Slate Pencil" Award, 1981.
Austrian Children's Book Award, 1984.

The High King

The John Newbery Medal, 1969.
National Book Award Finalist, 1969.
National Book Award Finalist, Paperback Fiction, 1981.

The Kestrel

>   Parent's Choice Award (Literature), 1982.
>   American Book Award Finalist, 1983.

The Marvelous Misadventures of Sebastian

>   The National Book Award, 1971.

The Town Cats

>   Norwegian Children's Book Prize, 1987.

Westmark

>   The American Book Award (formerly the National Book Award), 1982.

The Wizard in the Tree

>   National Book Award Finalist, 1976.

Awards for Contributions to Children's Literature

>   The Drexel Award, 1972.
>   Pennsylvania School Librarians, 1976.
>   Keystone State Reading Association, 1982.
>   The Swedish "Golden Cat" Award, 1984.
>   Citation by the Pennsylvania House of Representatives, 1985.
>   The Regina Medal of the Catholic Library Association, 1986.
>   Helen Keating Ott Award of the Church and Synagogue Library
>   Association, 1987.
>   Carolyn W. Field Award of the Pennsylvania Library Association, 1987.
>   Villanova University, 1990.

Other Awards

>   *Writer's Digest* Short Story Contest finalist, 1942.

APPENDIX II:
LLOYD ALEXANDER
CHRONOLOGY

1924	Born in Philadelphia on January 30.
1940	Graduated from Upper Darby High School.
	First job, messenger at Fidelity Philadelphia Trust Company.
1942	Dropped out of West Chester State Teachers' College.
	Began work at Atlantic Refining.
	Writer's Digest Short Story Contest finalist.
1943	Joined U. S. Army.
1944	Stationed in Britain and France during World War II.
1945	Enrolled in Sorbonne (Paris) after World War II.
	Met Paul Eluard and Gertrude Stein.
	Began translations of Eluard's work.
1946	Married Janine Denni.
	Returned to Philadelphia.
	Wrote the unpublished novel, *Another Country*.
	Began writing the unpublished novel, *Eden*.
1947	Commissioned to translate the work of Jean-Paul Sartre.
	Began writing the unpublished novel, *The Beautiful Children*.
1948	Employed by Sun Oil Company as an advertising copywriter.
1949	Translations of Sartre's *Nause* and *The Wall* published.
1951	Translation of Eluard's poetry in *Selected Writings* published.
	Moved to new home in Drexel Hill.
	Fired by Sun Oil.
1954	Wrote and sold first novel, *And Let the Credit Go*.
1955	*And Let the Credit Go* published.
1956	*My Five Tigers* published.

1958   First book for young readers, *Border Hawk*, published and awarded the National Jewish Book Award.
1959   *Janine is French* published.
1960   *My Love Affair with Music* published.
1961   *Flagship Hope* published.
1962   *Park Avenue Vet* published.
1963   *Time Cat* published, first fictional work for young readers.
        Long association with editor Ann Durell begins.
        Hired by Delaware Valley Announcer Magazine.
1964   *Fifty Years in the Doghouse* published.
        The Book of Three published.
1965   *The Black Cauldron* published.
        Coll and His White Pig published.
1966   *Castle of Llyr* published.
        The Black Cauldron named a Newbery Honor Book.
1967   *Taran Wanderer* published.
        The Truthful Harp published.
        Moved to current residence in Drexel Hill.
1968   *The High King* published.
1969   *The High King* receives the Newbery Medal and is a National Book Award finalist.
1970   *The Marvelous Misadventures of Sebastian* published.
1971   The National Book Award for Juvenile Literature is presented for *The Marvelous Misadventures of Sebastian*.
        The King's Fountain published.
        Author in residence at Temple University (1971-1974).
1972   Received Drexel Award for contributions to children's literature.
        The Four Donkeys published.
1973   *The Foundling* published.
        The Cat Who Wished to be a Man published and wins Boston Globe-Horn Book Honors for Fiction.
1975   *The Wizard in the Tree* published.
1976   National Book Award finalist for *The Wizard in the Tree*.
        Pennsylvania School Librarians Award for contributions to children's literature.
1977   *The Town Cats* published.
1978   *The First Two Lives of Lukas-Kasha* published.
1979   National Book Award Finalist and CRABbery Award for *The First Two Lives of Lukas-Kasha*.
1981   *Westmark* published.
        The Dutch "Silver Slate Pencil" Award for *The First Two Lives of Lukas-Kasha*.
        National Book Award Finalist, Paperback Fiction, for *The High King*.
1982   *The Kestrel* published.
        Westmark wins the American Book Award (formerly called the National Book Award).
        Parent's Choice Award for *The Kestrel*.

	Keystone State Reading Association Award for contributions to children's literature.
1983	American Book Award finalist for *The Kestrel*.
1984	*The Beggar Queen* is published.
1984	Swedish "Golden Cat" Award for contributions to children's literature.
	Austrian Children's Book Award for *The First Two Lives of Lukas-Kasha*.
1985	Walt Disney Productions releases the full length, animated film of *The Black Cauldron*
	Citation by Pennsylvania House of Representatives.
1986	*The Illyrian Adventure* published.
	Regina Medal of the Catholic Library Association for contributions to children's literature.
1987	*The El Dorado Adventure* published.
	Helen Keating Ott Award for contributions to children's literature.
	Carolyn W. Field Award for *The Illyrian Adventure*.
	Norwegian Children's Book Prize for *The Town Cats*.
1988	*The Drackenberg Adventure* published.
1989	*The Jedera Adventure* published.
1990	*The Philadelphia Adventure* published.
	Citation by Villanova University.

INDEX

McMillen, Dorothy: C31, **70**
"Meet the Author: Lloyd Alexander.": AV12, **120**
"Meet the Newbery Author Filmstrip Series: Lloyd Alexander.": AV11, **119**
"Meet Your Author.": C32, **70**; W25, **58**
"Meet Your Author: Lloyd Alexander (Who Wrote Dream-of-Jade).": W27, **58**
Melville, Herman: **2**
Michigan Librarian: W34, **59**
"Miklan Tells a Tale: The Pearls and the Pie.": S16, **51**
Miklovic, Janice: D5, **65**
Miller, Catharine K.: R26, **77**
Miller, Margaret H.: R226, **98**
Miller, Sara: R250, **101**; R364, **112**
Monico, David: R77, **82**
Monson, Diane: R143, **89**
Moore, Teresa: R289, **105**; R399, **116**; R44, **79**
More Books by More People: C21, **68**
Mosel, Arlene: R129, **88**
Mozart, Wolfgang Amadeus: **28**
Murphy, Bill: C33, **70**
"My Friend Rembrandt, Part I.": S18, **51**
"My Friend Rembrandt, Part II.": S19, **51**
"My Friend Rembrandt, Part III.": S20, **52**
"My Friend Rembrandt, Part IV.": S21, **52**
My Five Tigers: **17, 18, 29**; A4, **38**; F116, **48**; F37, **45**; F8, **44**
My Love Affair with Music: **18, 19**; A5, **38**; F62, **46**; F9, **44**
Mythlore: C38, **71**; M2, **120**
Myvyrian Archaiology: **22**

Nabokov, Vladimir: R418, **118**
National Book Award: **3, 30, 33**
National Jewish Book Award: **19**
National Observer: R100, **85**; R228, **98**; R377, **114**
"The Natures and Uses of Fantasy.": U10, **63**
Nausea: **13, 14**; T3, **44**
"NBA Winner Stresses Seriousness of Fantasy.": C34, **70**
Nebraska Library Association Quarterly: W34, **59**
Ness, Evaline: **27**
The New Advocate: C47, **73**; I3, **62**; R137, **88**; R152, **90**; W9, **55**
New Catholic World: R78, **82**
New Cumberland, Pennsylvania: **8**
New Directions for Women: R45, **79**
New Directions in Prose and Poetry Annual No. 10: T2, **43**
New Directions in Prose and Poetry Annual No. 11: S8, **50**
New Directions Press: **10, 12, 13**
New Statesman: R355, **112**
New Yorker: R11, **75**; R18, **76**; R116, **86**; R130, **88**
New York Herald Tribune Book Review: R5, **74**; R12, **75**; R24, **77**; R351, **111**
New York Review of Books: R79, **82**

About the Authors

JAMES S. JACOBS is Assistant Professor of Education at Brigham Young University, specializing in children's literature. He is especially fascinated with the Lloyd Alexander genre. At the time this book went to press, he was on sabbatical in Karlsruhe, Germany, teaching at an elementary school on an American military base.

MICHAEL O. TUNNELL is Assistant Professor in the Department of Curriculum and Instruction at Northern Illinois University. He is the author of *The Prydain Companion: A Reference Guide to Lloyd Alexander's Prydain Chronicles* (Greenwood, 1989) and articles in education and literary journals.

www.ingramcontent.com/pod-product-compliance
Lightning Source LLC
Chambersburg PA
CBHW070442100426
42812CB00004B/1186